"Two key challenges arise in ministering to North Korean defectors. First, South Korean Christians struggle to adapt to the shifting realities of defection. Second, a deeper issue concerns how those raised under Juche ideology and Kimilsungism experience conversion to Christianity. Dr. Keum explores both in her research, offering valuable insights for engaging North Koreans with the Gospel and equipping those involved in this ministry."

—BEN TORREY, Director, The Fourth River Project, Inc., Korea

"In this insightful study, Dr. Keum explores the spiritual journey of North Korean defectors in their transition from Juche ideology to a biblical worldview. By unveiling the factors of their challenges and overcoming them in internalizing God's Word, the work offers profound understanding and practical guidance for fostering discipleship and transformative faith. This book significantly contributes to those invested in the spiritual growth of North Korean believers and the church's mission."

—EIKO TAKAMIZAWA, Mongol Kids' Home, Japan

"Dr. Keum provides a rare, insider's look into the lives of North Korean Christian defectors. Through firsthand accounts, we see their disillusionment with failed ideologies and the North Korean regime, as well as the supernatural ways God gave them hope and purpose—some even returning despite the risk of persecution and death. Her research reveals that God's witness is present even within North Korea, where many encountered the Gospel before defecting. I highly endorse this study for its deep insights into North Korean lives and its relevance for future ministry."

—JAMIE KIM, Director, Reah International, USA

"Dr. Keum presents a significant theoretical framework of worldview change. Her study shows how grounded theory can construct a paradigm and theory using only inductive data analysis. This book will be a valuable resource to those who want to study the worldview change of any people group."

—CHANG SUP KANG, Professor, Grace Mission University, USA

"Dr. Keum has long held a deep compassion for North Korean defectors, dedicating herself to both their ministry and academic research. Her work focuses on the transformative power of the Gospel in reshaping their worldview—guiding them from the depths of one of the darkest regimes on earth into the marvelous light of God's kingdom. This insightful study not only sheds light on their journey but also serves as a valuable resource for future research and ministry. May this book illuminate the hearts of its readers and inspire deeper engagement with this crucial mission!"

—HYUNG JIN PARK, Professor, Torch Trinity Graduate University, South Korea

From Juche to Jesus

Evangelical Missiological Society Monograph Series

Anthony Casey, Rochelle Scheuermann, and Edward L. Smither
SERIES EDITORS

A Project of the Evangelical Missiological Society
www.emsweb.org

The EMS Monograph Series publishes the best book-length works of EMS members. The monographs may be reworked dissertations or original works based on missiological research focused on aspects of history, theology, culture, strategy, or spiritual formation all relating to the academic and practical nature of the missionary enterprise. EMS monographs are peer-reviewed and authors work with an editing team from Pickwick Publications (Wipf and Stock). Typically, 3–5 monographs are published each year.

From Juche to Jesus

A Study of Worldview Transformation Among North Korean Defector Christians in South Korea

Su Hwa Keum

☙PICKWICK *Publications* · Eugene, Oregon

FROM JUCHE TO JESUS
A Study of Worldview Transformation Among North Korean Defector Christians in South Korea

Evangelical Missiological Monograph Series 23

Copyright © 2025 Su Hwa Keum. All rights reserved. Except for brief quotations in critical publications or reviews, no part of this book may be reproduced in any manner without prior written permission from the publisher. Write: Permissions, Wipf and Stock Publishers, 199 W. 8th Ave., Suite 3, Eugene, OR 97401.

Pickwick Publications
An Imprint of Wipf and Stock Publishers
199 W. 8th Ave., Suite 3
Eugene, OR 97401

www.wipfandstock.com

PAPERBACK ISBN: 979-8-3852-2462-3
HARDCOVER ISBN: 979-8-3852-2463-0
EBOOK ISBN: 979-8-3852-2464-7

Cataloguing-in-Publication data:

Names: Keum, Su Hwa, author.

Title: From Juche to Jesus : a study of worldview transformation among North Korean defector Christians in South Korea / Su Hwa Keum.

Description: Eugene, OR: Pickwick Publications, 2025. | Evangelical Missiological Monograph Series 23. | Includes bibliographical references.

Identifiers: ISBN 979-8-3852-2462-3 (paperback). | ISBN 979-8-3852-2463-0 (hardcover). | ISBN 979-8-3852-2464-7 (ebook).

Subjects: LCSH: Missions. | Conversion. | Ideology. | Korea (North). | Self-reliance—Korea (North).

Classification: BL639 K2025 43 (print). | BL639 (epub).

07/10/25

All Scripture quotations are taken from the Holy Bible, New International Version®, NIV®. Copyright ©1973, 1978, 1984, 2011 by Biblica, Inc.™ All rights reserved worldwide. www.zondervan.com.

To my Lord Jesus, who is my guide and strength,
to my beloved parents in heaven, whose love continues to inspire me,
and to my dear friends, who walk this journey with me.

Contents

List of Tables, Diagrams, and Figures | ix
Preface | xi
Acknowledgments | xiii
List of Abbreviations | xv

1. Introduction | 1
2. Precedent and Related Literature | 10
3. Research Methodology | 44
4. Findings | 54
5. Conclusion | 168

Appendix A: Consent Form | 179
Appendix B: Demographic Questionnaire | 180
Bibliography | 181

List of Tables, Diagrams, and Figures

Table 1. The Change of Terms for North Korean Defectors | 13

Table 2. North Korean Defectors' Entry to South Korea (~Dec. 2024) | 13

Table 3. South Korean Government's Settlement Aid for North Korean Defectors | 16

Table 4. The Development Process of Juche Ideology | 22

Table 5. An Example of Memos: Check Points/Questions Raised on the Interview Data | 50

Screenshot 1. Analysis Memos on Participants Using Microsoft Word | 51

Table 6. Demographic Profile of Interview Participants | 55

Table 7. Themes and Subthemes of Life Prior to Conversion | 56

Table 8. Themes and Subthemes of Motives of Conversion | 71

Table 9. Themes and Subthemes of Immediate Changes Following the Conversion | 89

Table 10. Themes and Subthemes of Life after Conversion | 96

Table 11. Theme and Subthemes of Growth in Understanding of God, His Will, and Perspectives | 115

Table 12. Theme and Subthemes of Experiencing God | 129

List of Tables, Diagrams, and Figures

Diagram 1. Comparing Life Prior to Conversion with Conversion Motives | 145

Diagram 2. Comparing Life Prior to Conversion with Life after Conversion | 146

Diagram 3. Comparing Receiving Enlightenment with Repentance for Renewal | 148

Diagram 4. Comparing Receiving Enlightenment and Knowledge of God with Facing Challenges and Longing for Transformation | 149

Diagram 5. Comparing Receiving Enlightenment, Repentance for Renewal, Facing Challenges, and Experiencing God through His Word | 150

Diagram 6. Comparing Receiving Enlightenment, Internalization, and Experiencing God through the Word | 151

Diagram 7. Comparing Receiving Enlightenment, Experiencing God through the Word, and Evidence of Transformation | 153

Figure 1. Factors Influencing Worldview Transformation and Its Process: Insights from Themes and Categories Grounded in the Collected Data | 155

Diagram 8. The Process of Worldview Transformation & Correlation among the Key Factors | 156

Figure 2. The Dynamics of God's Word in the Transformation Process | 159

Figure 3. Paradigm Model according to Worldview Transformation Phenomenon | 165

Preface

THIS STUDY WAS BORN out of a deep concern for the spiritual journeys of North Korean defectors in South Korea. Having listened to many defectors' great testimonies of encountering the LORD during their difficult transitions, it became clear that, despite these profound encounters, many still distance themselves from the church once settled in South Korea. This troubling trend led me to question the depth of their conversion—specifically at the level of worldview.

As of December 2024, over 34,000 North Korean defectors have entered South Korea, though the numbers have been steadily declining since 2012. The impact of regime changes in North Korea, stricter border controls, and the effects of the COVID-19 pandemic have all played a part in this decline. While fewer defectors are arriving, it remains crucial to focus on those already settled in South Korea, helping them cultivate a strong biblical worldview and fully embrace God's kingdom. Through engaging in numerous conversations with defectors, I had the privilege of witnessing firsthand the profound spiritual changes they experienced. What I learned is that their journey of faith is not merely a shift in religious affiliation, but a deep, transformative process that reshapes their entire being.

Given the limited research on this topic, I turned to grounded theory to uncover the factors and processes behind the worldview transformation of these defectors. In doing so, I identified several obstacles to their transformation into a biblical worldview, including the lingering effects of Juche ideology, challenges of life in South Korea, and personal struggles. Despite these barriers, one of the key discoveries of this study is the central concept for genuine worldview transformation: *Experiencing God through the Word*. This transformation begins with an awakening to God's presence, often through personal crises, Bible reading, prayer, or sudden realizations, and deepens as individuals internalize his Word.

As the defectors' relationship with God deepens, their hearts are realigned, guiding them toward a biblical worldview. This transformation, as described by Charles Kraft through the *kingdom paradigm* or *Jesus' paradigm*, highlights the necessity of inner transformation that is rooted in God's rule and his love. Similarly, Jesus' reference to the *rock* upon which the church is built (Matt 16:18) underscores the foundation of this transformation. For these defectors, as for all of us, it is only when Christ truly reigns in our hearts that his kingdom can be established within us.

I have been deeply encouraged by the faith of those I studied, witnessing them embrace the love of Christ and strive to live under his reign. It is my hope that this book will help others see how God guides souls, allowing his kingdom and divine perspectives to take root in our hearts and transform our worldview. My prayer is that this work will inspire many to prioritize their relationship with Christ, embracing his love and entering into deeper fellowship with him. Only through this ongoing transformation of our worldview can Christ's kingdom be truly manifested in our lives and shared with the world around us.

Acknowledgments

"The one who began a good work in you will carry it on to completion until the day of Christ Jesus" (Phil 1:6). Truly, God is the ultimate source and driving force behind this work. I am sincerely humbled by his faithful guidance, wisdom, and grace, which have propelled me to embark on and diligently pursue this endeavor. I wholeheartedly acknowledge that all credit and glory rightly belong to him, for he has skillfully orchestrated his good work not only in my life but also in guiding the process of writing this paper.

Indeed, God has been the true initiator of this work, and he has graciously utilized numerous precious individuals to assist, guide, cherish, and support this endeavor. First and foremost, I am grateful to Dr. Chang Sup Kang, who was once my colleague and later became my advisor. His dedication to the kingdom, sacrificial spirit, and sincere commitment to God's work have been exemplary and deserving of recognition. I would also like to express my gratitude to my previous advisor, Dr. Eiko Takamizawa, who is no longer in Korea. However, her passion for God's kingdom provided me with invaluable support during the early stages of this paper. My department professors, Dr. Hyung Jin Park and Dr. Ah Young Kim, have consistently been there to offer me unwavering support. Their guidance, encouragement, and prayers have been invaluable sources of comfort and motivation that have propelled me to persevere in my studies. Without their care and dedication, attaining this level of completion in my study would have been an insurmountable challenge. I would also like to express my gratitude to Dr. Kyung Hwa Hong and Dr. Seung-Hyun Chung for their invaluable insights and contributions that have greatly enhanced the quality

Acknowledgments

and depth of my work. I also give my heartfelt appreciation to Dr. Miyon Chung, who is no longer with us at Torch Trinity. Her constant support and deep insights rooted in her systematic theological background have been instrumental in shaping and enriching my research.

I would like to dedicate a special acknowledgment to my parents, who are no longer with me. Despite their physical absence, I believe they rejoiced with me in advance and continue to do so in heaven. Additionally, I eagerly anticipate the day when my siblings come to know Jesus Christ. I am confident that when they grasp the grace and richness of my Lord Jesus Christ, they, too, will join in the joyous celebration. I am immensely grateful to my friends and co-workers who have stood by me through thick and thin, supporting me with their prayers, words of encouragement, and unwavering support. It is challenging to find adequate words to express my gratitude for their steadfast presence in my life. In particular, I would like to extend a heartfelt appreciation to my missionary friends, Jong Hoon Lee and Hyun Soon Kwon, Rev. Yeon Hee Chung, Rev. Yong Dae Kim, and his wife, Joo Yun Choi. May the Lord abundantly bless them for their kindness, generosity, and continued support. I appreciated the 20 participants who gladly shared their stories with God. They truly challenged, humbled, and blessed me. May the Lord receive glory from them.

Undoubtedly, this journey with God has been awe-inspiring in every way. It is impossible to express fully the magnitude of this experience in mere words. Throughout this journey, God has revealed his true nature to me, unveiling his limitless love and unwavering care. I am constantly reminded that through him, all things are possible, as he is the ultimate source of strength. LORD Jesus, your awesomeness knows no bounds, and I offer you all the glory and praise!

Abbreviations

DTS	Discipleship Training School
IOM	International Organization for Migration
IRB	Institutional Review Board
KINU	Korea Institute for National Unification
KWP	Korean Workers' Party
NIS	National Intelligence Service
NKDB	North Korean Data Base
NLL	Northern Limit Line
PTSD	Post-Traumatic Stress Disorder
SPN	Seoul Pyongyang News
UNHCR	United Nations High Commission for Refugees
WPK	Workers' Party of Korea

1

Introduction

Statement of Research Problem

As of December 2024, statistics from the Department of Unification indicated that 34,314 North Korean defectors had arrived in South Korea.[1] Since 2012, however, there has been a noticeable decline in the number of individuals leaving North Korea and entering South Korea, with only nineteen arrivals recorded from January to June 2022. This represents a sharp decrease compared to the trends observed over the past three decades. This reduction correlates with the transition in North Korea's government in 2010 and the impact of the COVID-19 pandemic. Andrei Lankov observed in 2022 that the number of defectors had nearly disappeared.[2] In light of these changes, Eui-Hyuck Kim emphasized the importance of shifting the focus of missions related to North Korean defectors from newly arriving individuals to those already residing in South Korea.[3]

Research on North Korean defectors who have settled in South Korea has primarily centered on their assimilation and adjustment, cultural shifts in behavior and values, and conversion to Christianity. However, limited attention has been given to the extent of worldview-level changes among defectors. According to Paul Hiebert, "if worldview is not transformed, in

---

1. Ministry of Unification, "Recent Status."
2. Andrei Lankov, "[Lankov]."
3. Eui-Hyuck, Kim, "Christian Missions," 84–112.

the long run the gospel is subverted and becomes captive to the local culture" and "the result is syncretistic Christo-paganism, which has the form but not the essence of Christianity."[4]

Reports have highlighted issues with the faith journeys of defector Christians, including many leaving the church after arriving in South Korea despite having accepted the gospel in transit nations. These observations underscore the importance of examining the conversion of North Korean defectors through the lens of worldview transformation. This focus is particularly relevant given that Juche ideology represents their overarching worldview.

Statement of Purpose

The biblical view of transformation involves a definitive moment of change and an ongoing process of growth and renewal; it is "both a point and a process."[5] In the context of worldview-level changes, certain factors play an important role, with these changes typically occurring more gradually than surface-level cultural adaptations. This gradual process can be attributed to the subconscious nature of worldview shifts, which progressively influence beliefs, values, and perceptions. A genuine transformative shift involves three cultural elements of cognition, affect, and evaluation.

The objective of this research is to develop a theoretical framework for understanding the factors and processes in transforming the worldviews of North Korean Christian defectors into a biblical worldview. North Koreans are widely recognized for their adherence to the Juche ideology, which may present significant challenges to this transformation. Therefore, this study aims to examine the process by which the worldviews of North Korean Christian defectors change, and to identify the factors that facilitate this process during their conversion and spiritual growth.

Research and Interview Questions

The research question is: What are the factors and processes involved in the worldview transformation of North Korean defector Christians living in South Korea? By identifying these factors and processes using the

---

4. Hiebert, *Transforming Worldviews*, 315.
5. Hiebert, *Transforming Worldviews*, 310, 316, 312.

Introduction

Grounded Theory methodology, this study aims to develop a theory of worldview transformation. The theoretical sampling process involves using insights from prior data collection and analysis to guide the selection of subsequent participants and data sources. Initially, however, the researcher will begin with the following open-ended questions to effectively guide the interviews:

1. What was your life like before you came to Christ?
2. What were your motives for converting to Christianity?
3. In what ways did your life change after your conversion?
4. What areas of your life have you found challenging to transform since your conversion?
5. How did you overcome these difficulties?
6. How did the transformation of your worldview into a Christian perspective occur?

Definition of Terms

The following are the definitions of essential terms used in this research:

Worldview: A worldview refers to the framework through which individuals or groups interpret life and the world around them. It comprises underlying "cognitive, affective, and evaluative assumptions" that provide meaning and guide the understanding of reality.[6] A worldview addresses fundamental questions such as: "What is the nature of humanity?" "What happens after death?" "What constitutes genuine reality?" and "How do we perceive the world we see?"[7]

Biblical Worldview: A biblical worldview, also referred to as the Kingdom perspective or Jesus' perspective, embodies the principles of "God's ways and thoughts" as revealed in Scripture (Isa 55:8–9; Exod 33:13, 18). It is rooted in the teachings and truths of the Bible and emphasizes a God-centered understanding of life and reality.

Transformation: Transformation involves a profound shift from preconceptions about life and the world to aligning with biblical truth. This process is often gradual and enduring, requiring intentional discipleship.

---

6. Hiebert, *Transforming Worldviews*, 25.
7. Sire, *Naming the Elephant*, 134–5.

Transformation seeks to conform every aspect of a person's life to the likeness of Christ Jesus.

Worldview Transformation into a Biblical Worldview: Worldview transformation, as defined by Hiebert, involves a comprehensive restructuring of cognitive, affective, and evaluative assumptions. The term *view* in worldview signifies a broad framework rather than a single perspective. Transformation into a biblical worldview entails aligning one's worldview with the vision and principles of the Kingdom of God, governed by Jesus Christ as King, with his Word as the guiding authority. Authentic transformation emphasizes the recognition and acceptance of the LORD Christ's Kingship, manifested in the believer's life through adherence to biblical principles.

Conversion to Christ: Conversion to Christ is defined as a relational turning away from evil or the worship of other gods to follow Christ (Acts 14:15; 1 Thess 1:9). This process includes repentance, baptism, and a commitment to live according to Christ's teachings. Conversion is marked by a reorientation of one's life towards Christ and his ways.

Juche: Juche is the political ideology comprising "the policies of self-reliance and independence that have guided the Democratic People's Republic of Korea (DPRK) since 1955."[8] It is based on two core principles: "[P]eople are the masters of their destiny," and they should remain free from external influence.[9]

Arduous March: This was a slogan introduced by Kim Jong Il following the death of Kim Il Sung in 1994 to inspire the willpower of the North Korean people to overcome severe economic hardships. The term draws on the historical narrative of Kim Il Sung's anti-Japanese guerrilla march in 1938, during which fighters endured extreme cold, hunger, and hardship for one hundred days to evade Japanese suppression operations in Manchuria.[10]

Disciple of Jesus Christ: A disciple of Jesus Christ is an individual who commits to following Jesus by prioritizing obedience to his Word, will, ways, thoughts, purposes, desires, and values. A disciple of Christ strives to imitate Christ's character and align every aspect of life with his teachings and example.

---

8. Hoare, *Historical Dictionary*, 191–92.

9. Hoare, *Historical Dictionary*, 191–92.

10. KBS World, "Arduous Journey." Kim Il Sung, Kim Jong Il, and Kim Jong Un are referred to in this way because it aligns with their common presentation in international media. All other names follow the Western convention of placing the first name before the last name.

Introduction

Assumptions for Research

The following are the assumptions underpinning the study:

1. Participant Integrity: Participants will provide honest responses and share their personal stories to the best of their knowledge. Furthermore, their involvement in the research will not result in harm or adverse consequences. This assumption is critical for fostering an environment of openness and authenticity, enabling a trustworthy exchange of information between the researcher and participants.

2. Religious Freedom in South Korea: North Korean defectors who have resettled in South Korea are presumed to have the freedom to engage in religious activities, such as attending church, participating in Bible study, and joining Christian fellowship. This assumption is based on South Korea's constitutional guarantee of religious freedom and the supportive environment it offers for individuals to practice their faith.

3. Participant Recommendation Criteria: The Christian defectors selected for interviews are recommended by their leaders and colleagues based on observable changes in their beliefs, values, and behaviors, rather than solely on the duration of their Christian journey. This underscores the emphasis on personal growth, character development, and the tangible application of faith within the community.

4. Reliability of Recommendations: The evaluations provided by the participants' leaders and colleagues in recommending them for the study are assumed to be reliable and credible.

5. Participant Motivation: Participants approach the interviews with sincere intent to support work related to North Korea that aligns with the researcher's objectives.

6. Residual Influence of the Juche Worldview: Despite their conversion experiences and physical relocation from North Korea, participants are presumed to remain under the residual influence of the Juche worldview. Given that worldviews are often formed unconsciously from birth, it is anticipated that achieving a profound transformation at the worldview level will require significant time and ongoing discipleship.

7. Role of External Influences in Conversion: The majority of participants are expected to have experienced conversion in the context of desperate circumstances, where their immediate needs were met

through interactions with believers or in mission homes managed by missionaries in transit countries. Consequently, their conversion motivations may have been influenced not only by God but also by the values and beliefs of those mediating the gospel.

8. Authenticity of Shared Changes: The changes shared by participants may not always reflect a genuine transformation toward a biblical worldview. Authentic worldview transformation is initiated and sustained by God and his Word. This process is divinely orchestrated, with God reigning through his Word as the ultimate authority. Consequently, changes that do not stem from God's guidance cannot be regarded as true transformations aligned with a biblical worldview. Such changes remain incompatible with the principles of God's Kingdom, where "every Word that comes from the mouth of God" (Matt 4:4) serves as the foundation of its law and values. True transformation is, therefore, a work initiated by God himself.

9. Authority and Sufficiency of the Bible: The Bible is the inerrant Word of God, without error, and sufficient for transforming lives. Under the influence of the Holy Spirit, the Bible holds the power to bring about meaningful and lasting changes in individuals' lives.

Significance of Research

This study is significant for several reasons:

1. Strategizing Missional Activity: North Koreans often perceive Christianity as a foreign influence and a threat to Juche ideology. Understanding the factors and processes involved in the worldview transformation of North Korean defector Christians can help inform strategies for effective missional work among this population.

2. Enhancing Cross-Cultural Understanding: This research can provide South Korean churches with a deeper understanding of the unique worldviews of North Korean defectors, shaped by over 70 years of separation. Such insights will enable churches to approach defectors with respect and from a cross-cultural perspective, fostering more effective engagement and ministry.

3. Strengthening Faith Amid Challenges: For North Korean defector Christians who may experience weakening of their faith, the findings

of this study can offer pathways to a deeper conversion, including a transformative shift in worldview. By applying the identified factors and processes of worldview change, churches and ministries can better support the spiritual growth and perseverance of these individuals.

4. Guiding Discipleship Efforts: Analyzing the processes of worldview transformation can provide valuable insights for discipleship efforts within the church. These insights can help identify the key requirements for facilitating complete and lasting transformation in believers, thereby strengthening the church's mission and ministry.

Delimitations

1. Participant Selection: The research limits its scope to 20 North Korean defector Christians who have undergone a significant shift in their worldview, as assessed and approved by their leaders and/or peers.

2. Influence of Participant Perspectives: The study acknowledges that participants' experiences of worldview transformation are influenced by their own perspectives and interpretations of events.

3. Focus on Biblical Worldview Transformation: While external factors such as globalization may impact participants' transformations following their defection, this research specifically focuses on the characteristics and process of their transformation into a biblical worldview.

4. Research Approach and Framework: This study employs an inductive approach to investigate participants' experiences of worldview transformation. Recognizing that worldview transformation occurs not only at an individual level but also within societal, historical, and cultural contexts, the research adopts a social constructivist interpretive framework to analyze these dynamics.[11]

11. Chang Seop Kang emphasizes the importance of the researcher clearly articulating their philosophical stance when conducting research, as the researcher plays a central role in generating knowledge and shaping the phenomena observed during the research process. Providing a clear philosophical rationale enables readers to evaluate the study from the researcher's perspective. Creswell and Poth highlight that within the interpretive framework of social constructivism, the researcher's goal is "to understand the world in which the interviewees live and work." Additionally, its epistemological belief posits that "the reality is constructed between the researcher and the researched and shaped by individual experiences." See *Five Approaches*, 34–35.

Limitations

The study acknowledges the following limitations:

1. Language Nuances and Interpretation: Individual interviews with North Korean defector Christians serve as the primary research strategy. While participants speak Korean, there may be subtle differences in word meanings and nuances compared to the Korean spoken in South Korea. To address this, the researcher will exercise caution to ensure accurate interpretation of the interviews and precise translation of selected sections into English for inclusion in the report.
2. Subjectivity of Data: The data collected consists of participants' interview responses, which reflect their subjective perceptions of reality. These responses may not necessarily capture objective truths but are valuable for understanding the participants' lived experiences.
3. Generalizability of Findings: The theory developed through the Grounded Theory methodology is context-specific, reflecting the experiences of the study's participants. As such, the findings may not be universally generalizable but are intended to provide meaningful insights relevant to similar contexts or populations.

Methodology

Given the specific nature of this research, a qualitative research approach has been selected. Grounded Theory methodology will be employed to develop a theory regarding the factors and processes involved in the transformation of North Korean defector Christians' worldviews into a biblical one. The study will utilize open-ended interview questions to explore participants' experiences of worldview transformation, beginning from the moment of their conversion to the present.

The primary data source for this study will be interviews conducted with 20 North Korean defector Christians. Data analysis will be carried out using QSR's NVivo 12 software, which is designed for qualitative and mixed-methods research.[12] NVivo 12 aids in the conceptualization, categorization, and systematic analysis of qualitative data, supporting the organization of interview responses.

---

12. Kent State University, "NVIVO," para. 1.

Introduction

This study also draws on several key texts to guide its methodological approach, including John W. Creswell and Cheryl N. Poth's *Qualitative Inquiry and Research Design*,[13] Anselm Strauss and Juliet Corbin's *Basics of Qualitative Research: Techniques and Procedures for Developing Grounded Theory* (2nd and 3rd editions),[14] Kathy Charmaz's *Constructing Grounded Theory*,[15] and Chang Sup Kang's *Transforming Research Methodology for Missiology: A Practical Guide through Grounded Theory*.[16]

In the introduction to this study, the research problem, purpose, research and interview questions, definition of terms, assumptions, significance, delimitations, limitations, and methodology have been outlined. The next chapter will review the relevant literature to provide a foundation for the research and contextualize the study within existing body of scholarship.

---

13. Creswell, *Qualitative Inquiry*.
14. Strauss and Corbin, *Basics*.
15. Charmaz, *Grounded Theory*.
16. Chang Sup Kang, *Transforming Research*.

2

Precedent and Related Literature

THIS CHAPTER EXAMINES KEY themes relevant to the research and is organized into five sections. The first section provides an overview of North Korean defectors, exploring various aspects of their lives and their interactions with the South Korean church. The second section focuses on Juche ideology, the dominant worldview shaping the lives and beliefs of the North Korean people. The third section briefly examines the concept of conversion, emphasizing that it is not just a singular event but a process of ongoing transformation. Recognizing that complete transformation requires a shift in worldview, the fourth section introduces the concepts of worldview and worldview transformation, highlighting the foundational themes of a biblical worldview. The final section reviews the literature on research methodology, with a particular focus on qualitative research methods and Grounded Theory, which provide the methodological framework for this study.

Understanding North Korean Defectors

This section examines six key themes to provide a deeper understanding of North Korean defectors: the terminology used to describe them, recent developments in defection, their adjustment experiences in South Korea, the South Korean government's settlement aid initiatives, the relationship between South Korean churches and defectors, and previous studies on North Korean defectors' Christian faith.

Precedent and Related Literature

Terminology Used to Describe North Korean Defectors

Many terms have been used interchangeably to refer to North Korean defectors, each carrying distinct connotations. Scholars often use the term *diaspora* to describe a minority group that maintains a strong connection to their homeland through economic and emotional ties while preserving their national identity.[1] Alternatively, the term *migrant*, as defined by the International Organization for Migration (IOM), refers to "a person who moves away from his or her place of usual residence, whether within a country or across an international border, temporarily or permanently, and for a variety of reasons."[2] The *Cambridge Dictionary* further defines a migrant as "a person who travels to a different country or place, often in search of employment."[3]

The term *refugee* applies to individuals "who have fled war, violence, conflict, or persecution and have crossed an international border to seek safety in another country."[4] North Korean defectors share certain similarities with refugees, but this designation is not entirely accurate. Upon completing the settlement program at Hanawon, defectors become eligible for South Korean citizenship,[5] which distinguishes them from foreign refugees residing in South Korea.[6] The Chinese government, however, does not grant refugee status to North Korean defectors in China, citing the "China and North Korea Criminal Extradition Agreement" of 1960 and additional agreements in 1986 concerning the repatriation of illegal entrants and cooperation for national security and border preservation.[7] In contrast, since 2004, the United States of America has granted refugee status to 225 North Korean defectors (as of November 2022).[8] The United Kingdom provided

---

1. Young Sup Song, "Understanding North Korean," 139.
2. UN Migration, "'Migrant.'"
3. Cambridge Dictionary, "migrant."
4. UN Refugee Agency, "refuge?"
5. Hanawon, established in 1999, is a South Korean resettlement facility designed to help North Korean defectors transition into South Korean society. Funded by the Ministry of Unification (MOU), the facility functions as a combination of a halfway house, trade school, and reeducation center. All defectors are required to complete the program before fully integrating into South Korean society. This privilege is available exclusively to the North Korean defectors.
6. Jeon, Yoo, and Lee, "The Patterns," 1.
7. Park et al., *North Korean Diaspora*, 74.
8. Korea JoongAng Daily, "U.S."

refugee status to approximately 600 North Korean defectors as of 2014, although the number has declined significantly since 2008.[9]

A *North Korean defector* is an individual who has escaped from North Korea, maintains family, work, or other ties there, and has not acquired foreign nationality before arriving in South Korea. Upon expressing their intention to seek asylum, the South Korean government processes their claim and provides assistance to help them adapt and settle into society.[10]

In a broader context, the term *defector* typically refers to "someone who leaves a country, political party, etc., especially in order to join an opposing one."[11] Among related terms, *defector* and *refugee* carry strong political connotations, whereas *migrant* does not. It is crucial to distinguish between refugees and migrants, as these terms are not interchangeable and have significant legal differences. According to the United Nations High Commissioner for Refugees (UNHCR), "confusing these terms can result in difficulties for refugees and asylum-seekers, as well as misunderstandings in conversations about asylum and migration."[12] The UNHCR provides the following definitions of *migrant* and *refugee*:

> A uniform legal definition of the term 'migrant' does not exist at the international level. Some policymakers, international organizations, and media outlets understand and use the word 'migrant' as an umbrella term to cover both migrants and refugees. For instance, global statistics on international migration typically use a definition of 'international migration' that would include many asylum-seeker and refugee movements.[13]

The Korean Ministry of Unification has documented various terms used to refer to North Korean defectors, along with their chronological evolution, as shown in Table 1. Terms such as *Saeteomin* (used between 2005 and 2008) and *North Korean Repatriates* (used between 1994 and 1996) were commonly used. However, since 2008, the term *defector* has become increasingly prevalent. This shift in terminology aligns with the preference of the North Korean defector ministers' group, which has also endorsed this term. Consequently, this research will adopt the term *defector* as the standard term.

9. Right to Remain News, "UK."
10. Ministry of Unification, "Refugee Act."
11. Cambridge Dictionary, "Defector."
12. UN Refugee Agency, "'Refugees' and 'Migrants.'"
13. UN Refugee Agency, "'Refugees' and 'Migrants.'"

PRECEDENT AND RELATED LITERATURE

Table 1. The Change of Terms for North Korean Defectors[14]

Year & Period	Term(s)
After Mid-1990s	Defected North Korean Soldiers
1994–1996	Defector/Defected Ethnic North Korean
1997–2004	Defector/North Korean Defectors
2005–2008	*Saeteomin* (People in a New Place)/North Korean Defectors
After 2008	North Korean Defectors (Defector)

Current Development in Defection

As of December 2024, the total number of North Korean defectors in South Korea stands at 34,314 as shown in Table 2.[15] Following Kim Jong Un's rise to power in 2011, the number of defectors decreased by nearly half compared to previous years, primarily due to increased border security and harsher penalties for defection.[16] The numbers fell sharply again from 1,137 in 2018 and 1,047 in 2019 to just 229 in 2020. This sharp decline is largely attributed to the COVID-19 pandemic and the implementation of a stronger blockade by North Korea, which further tightened border controls. These factors have made defection increasingly difficult during this period.

Table 2. North Korean Defectors' Entry to South Korea (~Dec. 2024)[17]

Sex/Year	~'98	~'01	'02	'03	'04	'05	'06	'07
Male	831	565	510	474	626	424	515	573
Female	116	478	632	811	1,272	960	1,513	1,981
Total	947	1,043	1,142	1,285	1,898	1,384	2,028	2,554
Women (%)	12%	46%	55%	63%	67%	69%	75%	78%

14. Seong Jong Joo, *A Research*, 39.
15. Ministry of Unification, "Recent Status."
16. Robert King, "Defectors Declines." The UN Commission of Inquiry on DPRK human rights reported that defectors are deemed "to have committed 'treason against the Fatherland by defection' under the Criminal Code," a crime that is punished by a minimum of five years of "reform through labor." (COI Detailed findings, paragraphs 380–492.) North Korean border guards have orders to shoot illegal border crossers, and credible media reports clearly indicate that the border guards understand and fulfill those orders.
17. Ministry of Unification, "Recent Status."

Sex/Year	'08	'09	'10	'11	'12	'13	'14	'15	'16
Male	608	662	591	795	404	369	305	251	302
Female	2,195	2,252	1,811	1,911	1,098	1,145	1,092	1,024	1,116
Total	2,803	2,914	2,402	2,706	1,502	1,514	1,397	1,275	1,418
Women (%)	78.3%	77.3%	75.4%	70.6%	73%	76%	78%	80.3%	78.7%

Sex/Year	'17	'18	'19	'20	'21	'22	'23	*'24	TOTAL
Male	188	168	202	72	40	35	32	26	9,568
Female	939	969	845	157	23	32	164	210	24,746
Total	1,127	1,137	1,047	229	63	67	196	236	34,314
Women (%)	83.3%	85.2%	80.7%	68.6%	36.5%	47.8%	83.7%	89.0%	72.1%

Source: Ministry of Unification Statistics 2024 *tentative

1948: The first defection to the South

February 2007: The number of defectors reached 10,000 people

November 2010: The number of defectors reached 20,000 people

November 2016: The number of defectors reached 30,000 people

North Korean Defectors' Adjustment

When examining the adjustment of North Korean defectors to South Korean society, Eui-Hyuck Kim identifies several key variables: the time of defection from North Korea, the duration of stay in transit countries, and the time of arrival in South Korea.[18] He also notes that most defectors face similar challenges, particularly during their first 5 years of settlement.[19] In fact, major studies on North Korean defectors' adjustment to South Korean society, conducted from 1995 to 2008 (when the largest influx of defectors occurred in 2008 and 2009), identified several reasons for their maladjustment. These challenges remain largely consistent today, highlighting the enduring nature of the difficulties defectors continue to face during their settlement.

18. Eui-Hyuck Kim, "Understanding North Korean," 168–80.
19. Kim, "Understanding North Korean," 168–80.

Financial hardships are a common issue. Many defectors remit an average of 2.09 million won to family members in the North, incurring a 30 percent broker fee, according to the *2021 North Korean Defector Economic and Social Integration Status* published by the North Korean Database.[20] These remittances place a significant strain on their financial resources. Health issues are another major challenge. Defectors often suffer from internal diseases, chronic headaches, indigestion, and PTSD from their perilous journeys.[21] Maladjustment to their new environment can also lead to mental health problems such as "anxiety and depression from victimization, anger, lethargy, and reliance" or dependence on others."[22]

Employment poses additional difficulties.[23] Many defectors struggle with job acquisition and retention, as South Korean workplaces, such as factories or restaurants, often require intense labor that contrasts sharply with the looser socialist work system they were accustomed to. Combined with their poor health, this mismatch frequently results in high turnover rates during the early stages of settlement. Social integration is another significant hurdle. Defectors face difficulties adapting to South Korea's pluralistic society with its diverse political and social systems. Discrimination, indifference, and even well-intentioned but patronizing attitudes from South Koreans often lead to frustration.[24] While initial support is beneficial, a lack of reciprocal respect can undermine the defectors' sense of dignity and belonging. Despite these shared challenges, Eui-Hyuck Kim emphasizes the need to recognize and address each defector's unique circumstances, especially during the crucial first 5 years of settlement. Tailored support and a willingness to genuinely listen to their experiences can play a vital role in facilitating their successful adjustment to South Korean society.

South Korean Government Settlement Aid

The most recent South Korean government settlement funding allocated for North Korean defectors is presented in Table 3 below.

20. Adventist News, "Status of North Korean."
21. Jung Ho Kim, *The Issues*, 58.
22. Kyung Mi Kang, "Mal-Adjustment," 207.
23. Jung Ho Kim, *The Issues*, 58–59.
24. Eui-Hyuck Kim, "Understanding North Korean," 175.

Table 3. South Korean Government's Settlement Aid for North Korean Defectors[25]

Category	Item	Description
Settlement benefits	Basic benefits	KRW 8 million for a single-person household
	Financial incentives	A maximum of KRW 25.1 million for those who receive vocational training, obtain a certificate of qualification, or get a job
	Additional benefits	A maximum of KRW 15.4 million for seniors aged 60 years or older, the mentally or physically challenged, people in long-term medical treatment, children of single parents, and children born in third countries
Housing	Arrangement	Arranging rental apartments
	Subsidies	KRW 16 million for a single-person household
Employment	Training	A training allowance (Ministry of Employment and Labor)
	Employment subsidies (paid to employers)	Half of pay (up to half a million won) per worker for a maximum of four years Those who entered South Korea before November 29, 2014
	Support workers	Offering career counseling and job placement at 65 employment centers nationwide
	Others	Employment protection (preferential purchasing), settlement support for those aspiring to be farmers, and special employment
Social Welfare	Livelihood benefits	Those who receive Basic Livelihood Security Program (BLSP) benefits
	Medical care	Free healthcare for those who receive Tier 1 Medical Benefits of the BLSP
	Pension exception	Allowing subscription by exception to the national pension plan for those aged between 50 and 59 at the time of making decisions on protection
Education	Special admission & transfer to schools	Offering special admission for those who want to go to college
	Support for tuition	Exemption from tuition for those enrolled in middle school, high school, a national or public university and subsidizing 50% of tuition for study at a private university
Settlement assistants		Designating one or two settlement assistants for each household in the initial period of settlement Support workers
Support workers		Support workers system: community services (244 persons at local governments), employment counseling (65 persons at employment centers), and personal protection (900 persons at police stations)

25. Ministry of Unification, "Settlement Support."

Dynamics Between the Church and the Defectors

The relationship between South Korean churches and North Korean defectors is complex and multifaceted. According to recent research, as of May 2023, there are 68 defector churches in South Korea, with approximately 2,400 members.[26] Based on estimates, the ratio between defector believers and South Korean believers in these churches ranges from 8:2 to 6:4, placing the number of defector believers between 1,400 and 1,900. If the total number of defector Christians is approximately 10,000, only 14 to 19 percent attend defector churches. Of these, around 1,600–1,800 defectors are estimated to attend defector churches, while approximately 1,500 attend South Korean churches.[27] Meanwhile, the 2022 report by the Database Center for North Korean Human Rights noted that 41.4 percent of the 14,832 defectors interviewed identified as Christians. This suggests that there were over 13,000 defector Christians at that time. This indicates that around 10,000 defector Christians remain unchurched, often referred to as "Canaan Christians."[28]

Whether attending defector or South Korean churches, defector Christians face a variety of complex challenges. A 2023 study by *Kook Min Newspaper* identified three reasons why defectors leave churches: (1) churches offering financial support to defectors in exchange for their attendance, (2) pressure to attend frequent meetings despite their limited spiritual development, and (3) churches not accommodating their demanding work schedules, which often include Sundays.[29]

Eui-Hyuck Kim's research categorizes defector Christians' church experiences into three key areas.[30] The first, *discomfort due to familiar practices*, describes the unease defectors feel when church practices resemble aspects of North Korean culture. The second, *tension from conflicting beliefs*, occurs when biblical teachings clash with their Juche ideology and atheistic worldview. The third, *dissatisfaction with secular church culture*, arises when defectors view the church as just another aspect of broader South Korean society, adopting secular values without questioning them.

26. Hyung Shin Chung, "North Korean Mission."

27. The Mission, "Disillusioned."

28. The term "Canaan Christian" holds a unique meaning in Korean. When the word *Canaan* is read backward in Korean (*an-na-ca*), it translates to "people not going (to church)."

29. The Mission, "Disillusioned."

30. Eui-Hyuck Kim, "Migrants' Church Experiences," 177–8.

Beyond church-related dynamics, generational conflicts also arise. For instance, younger defectors in their 20s may perceive their first-generation Christian parents as excessively legalistic, equating their emphasis on faith with the ideological indoctrination they encountered in North Korea. This often heightens tensions between generations.[31]

To address these challenges, Young Sup Song advocates for South Korean churches to view defectors as part of a *diaspora* community.[32] He suggests that, like the Korean-Chinese community, North Korean defectors have formed a multicultural group with sociopolitical significance. By recognizing and valuing defectors' unique cultural backgrounds and experiences, as noted by Kim and Song, churches can create a more inclusive and accepting environment. This fosters a sense of belonging, enabling defectors to integrate into South Korean society while growing spiritually. This approach fosters a sense of belonging and acceptance, encouraging defectors to embrace their identity as Christians within the broader context of South Korean society.

Ben Torrey from Jesus Abbey underscores this idea, stating, "The greatest thing that the church can do is to accept the idea that North Korean migrants do not need to become South Koreans."[33] Similarly, Woo Taek Jeon, in his study "The Patterns and Formation of National Identity among North Korean Refugees in South Korea,"[34] emphasizes that defectors experience a more successful settlement process when they embrace their North Korean identity while also developing self-respect as South Korean citizens. By promoting this balance, churches can help defectors navigate their dual identities, empowering them to thrive in their new community without losing their sense of self.

Previous Studies on North Korean Defectors' Christian Faith

Research on the religious experiences and faith journeys of North Korean defectors has provided valuable insights into their spiritual transformation. A study by the North Korean Database (NKDB) found that 1.2 percent (163 out of 13,563 participants) reported attending religious meetings in secret

---

31. Jun, Park, and Cho, "Phenomenological Study," 245.
32. Young Sup Song, "Understanding North Korean," 139.
33. Torrey, "North Korean Migrants?," 12.
34. Jeon, Yu, and Lee, "The Patterns," 25.

while in North Korea.[35] Among them, 16 defectors who left the North before 2000 had read the Bible, representing just 0.12 percent, whereas 541 defectors who left after 2000 had read the Bible—a nearly 35-fold increase. According to the *White Paper on Religious Freedom 2020*, this rise is attributed to the influx of Bibles into North Korea, with the number of Bible readers increasing by 4 percent annually since 2000.

NKDB's *White Paper 2020* also explores where defectors first practiced religious activities. Among defectors currently practicing religion, 34.7 percent (3,544 individuals) began their religious journey in the National Intelligence Service,[36] 29.6 percent (3,022) in China, 26.8 percent (2,739) in Hanawon, 5.7 percent (584) in third-world countries other than China, and 1.7 percent (175) in North Korea.[37]

Early research (before 2021) on defectors' Christian faith often focused on comparisons between Christianity and the North Korean regime: Suk Hong Kim's "Study on the Similarity between Christianity and the North Korean System" (1999) and Byung Ro Kim's "Religiosity of North Korean Society: Comparison of Religious Forms between Juche Ideology and Christianity" (2000).[38] These two studies explore parallels and contrasts between the two systems. Byung Ro Kim's study, which is relevant to understanding the ideological divide between Juche and Christianity, will be discussed further in this chapter.

After 2000, studies began to examine defectors' conversion to Christianity in more depth. Young Ahm Kim's thesis, "Study on defectors' conversion into Christianity" (2001), denotes that the more Juche education defectors received in the North, the more hindrances they experienced in accepting the Christian faith. In other words, extensive Juche education created significant barriers to accepting the Christian faith. Ye Young Park's thesis, "Study on the religious experiences of North Korean Defector Christians" (2016), identifies three stages of conversion: "seeking God's experience," "struggle of faith," and "overcoming faith."[39] Her work identifies five types of struggles occurring in the struggle of faith stage: doubts about God, difficulties with other Christians, discontent with the Christian system,

---

35. Christianity Daily, "99.6% of Defectors."

36. National Intelligence Service is the investigation facility upon defectors' arrival in the South.

37. SPN, "NKDB 'Summary of 2020.'"

38. Byung Ro Kim, *Religiosity*.

39. Ye Young Park, "Conversion Experience," 94–110.

struggles with faith itself, and discomfort with the South Korean church's atmosphere.[40] Park's research highlights that while environmental factors such as attending church and building relationships with other Christians play an important role in spiritual growth, the most profound experience reported by defectors was discovering who God is and understanding the nature of the personal relationship each individual can have with him.

Myung-Hee Jun and his two colleagues further explored the conversion experiences of young North Korean defectors in their 2018 study, "Phenomenological study toward understanding the process of religious conversion of Christian young adults from North Korea: Through the phenomenological approach" (2018).[41] Using Rambo's theory and Colaizzi's method, the thesis outlines five stages of conversion for defectors in their 20s, most of whom were born or infants during the *Arduous March* of the 1990s.[42] Many second-generation defectors had already encountered the gospel through family members in North Korea, which reduced resistance to Christianity.[43] Their parents, already in South Korea, often prayed for them and facilitated their defection, leading participants to view their faith as divinely guided. Despite this, they experienced crises of faith, including conflicts arising from strict Christian education within their families. Ultimately, by God's grace, they developed a personal relationship with God, found peace in their identity, and renewed their sense of purpose as Christians and defectors.[44] The studies above significantly contribute to our understanding of the conversion process among North Korean defector Christians.

Studies on defectors' worldview transformation, though limited, offer additional insights. The following are especially noteworthy. Won Hak Oh's 1999 study, "The Study of Changes in the Worldview of North Korean Defectors," uses questionnaires to gather data from 35 defectors who had been in South Korea for one to three months. The study examines their perspectives on various topics, including humanity, society, the afterlife, religion, God, nature, the universe, and four central myths: the reunification

---

40. Park, "Conversion Experience," 110.

41. Jun, Park, and Cho, "Phenomenological Study," 245.

42. The *Arduous March* (1994–1998) or the *March of Suffering* refers a catastrophic period in North Korea marked by severe famine and economic collapse. See https://www.usip.org/publications/1999/08/politics-famine-north-korea, accessed January 8, 2025.

43. Myung-Hee Jun et al., "Phenomenological Study," 221.

44. Myung-Hee Jun et al., "Phenomenological Study," 221.

myth, paradise myth, victory myth, and liberation myth.[45] Although his study acknowledges that the short duration of their stay in the South limited its ability to produce statistically significant results regarding broader worldview changes, it notes that, even in this brief period, the defectors' perceptions of God, nature, and the universe underwent meaningful transformation.[46] Similarly, "A Qualitative Study of North Korean Refugees' Attitude Shifts: Focusing on Those in South Korea for Three Years," published in 2012 by Shieun Yu and colleagues, identifies changes in self-esteem, altruism, comparative perspectives, and religious attitudes over 3 years.[47] The study examines the transformation of attitudes among defectors.

For a deeper exploration of North Korean defectors' worldview, the 2016 study by Myung-Hee Jun and four other researchers, titled "A Qualitative Study Toward Understanding the Process of Religious Experiences of Christian North Korean Defectors: Through the Grounded Theory Approach," offers valuable insights into their religious experiences.[48] The study is based on interviews with 13 first-generation Christian defectors who had been practicing their faith for at least 3 years and identified as committed believers. The findings were analyzed using Strauss and Corbin's Grounded Theory model. The interview data yielded 20 categories and 96 subcategories, with the core category and central phenomenon identified as "an irresistible encounter with God as being."[49] Through their actions and interactions, the defectors' understanding of God deepened, allowing them to embrace his image, recognize the significance of their mission and purpose, and achieve a balanced integration of faith into their daily lives. When this research is considered alongside the two studies mentioned earlier and Ye Young Park's findings, it becomes evident that establishing a strong faith and cultivating a meaningful relationship with God for defectors is a process that requires both time and the grace of God. These studies collectively underscore the transformative journey of faith for defectors as they navigate their new spiritual and social realities.

So far, we have observed that various terms for defectors reflect different perspectives on their status and integration. While they face cultural, economic, and psychological challenges in South Korea, government

---

45. Woon Hak Oh, "Study of Changes," v.
46. Woon Hak Oh, "Study of Changes," vi.
47. Yu, Oh, et al., "Qualitative Study," 119.
48. Jun, Jung, et al., "Religious Experiences," 221.
49. Jun, Jung, et al., "Religious Experiences," 207.

programs like Hanawon, financial aid, and job training aim to support their resettlement, though gaps remain. Churches also play a key role in providing aid and community support, while previous studies have explored their adjustment experiences, identity transformation, and the role of faith in their integration. Building on this understanding of North Korean defectors, the next section will examine Juche ideology, which has shaped the beliefs and values of North Korean society.

Juche Ideology

Juche ideology stands as the cornerstone of North Korean thought, deeply influencing the worldview of its people. To truly understand the experiences and mindset of North Korean defectors, it is essential to explore the origins and evolution of Juche, focusing on its development, the mechanisms of its internalization, and the core doctrines that underpin this ideology.

Development of Juche

This section examines the origins and evolution of Juche ideology. Table 4 below outlines the development of Juche, highlighting its main components alongside the dates of discussion at the Korean Workers' Party (KWP) congresses and the corresponding historical context.

Table 4. The Development Process of Juche Ideology[50]

Content	Date	Historical Context
Ideological Self-Reliance	KWP* Congress on Propaganda and Agitation (Dec 28, 1955)	Stalin's death Elimination of *Namrodang* factions within KWP
Economic Self-Reliance	Full Congress of KWP Central Committee (Dec 11, 1956)	Reduction in foreign aid (5 years) Stagnation of economic planning Rising of anti-Kim movement within the party

50. Ministry of National, *Understanding North Korea 2013* (Seoul: Education Development Division, 2013), 29.

Precedent and Related Literature

Content	Date	Historical Context
Political Self-Reliance	Extended Full Congress of KWP Central Committee (Dec. 5, 1957)	Campaign against personal cults in the Communist Party Overthrow of coastal and Soviet factions within the party
Self-Defense	5th Full Congress of 4th KWP Central Committee (Dec. 10, 1962)	Intensification of China-Soviet conflict Seeking U.S.-Soviet coexistence South Korean 5·16 military upheaval
Diplomatic Self-Reliance	2nd Congress of KWP Representatives (Oct 5, 1966)	Escalation of China-Soviet conflicts Institution of non-alliance movements
Establishment of a Monolithic System of Thought	15th Full Congress of 4th KWP Central Committee (May 28, 1967) 8th Full Congress of 5th KWP Central Committee (Feb 12, 1974) National Propaganda Day lecture to the military (Feb 19, 1974)	Establishment of Kim Il Sung's one-man regime and his personal cult
Fortification of Juche Thought Throughout Society	6th Congress of the KWP (Oct. 10, 1980)	Consolidation of the father-son hereditary system
Juche Ideology, Ideologization of Monolithic Rule of Military-First	3rd Congress of KWP Representatives (28 September 2010)	Formalization of the three generations of succession
Ideologization of Kim Il-sung and Kim Jongilism's Monolithic Rule	4th Congress of KWP Representatives (11 April 2012)	Inauguration of Kim Jong Un's regime

*KWP: Korean Workers' Party

Juche ideology initially emphasized strong resistance to imperialism and the intrusion of foreign cultures. In the beginning, North Korea's Juche ideology aligned with Khrushchev's destalinization process, which criticized the one-man dictatorships established in the USSR and China. However, over time, Juche ideology evolved to solidify Kim Il-sung's leadership, framing the concept of self-reliance around the central role of the leader. This became a core part of the ideology, focusing on maintaining the dictatorship and promoting national sovereignty. On an international level, neutrality became both a diplomatic strategy and a political ideology, enabling North Korea to navigate the ideological conflict between China and the USSR while maintaining an independent stance.[51]

To understand the philosophical worldview underlying North Korean communism, it is essential to begin with its foundation in materialism,[52] which encompasses atheism and the theory of evolution.[53] Christian theism was reinterpreted within a philosophical framework by G.W.F. Hegel (1770–1831), who viewed God as the Absolute Spirit and saw history as the unfolding of this spirit through human events.[54] One of Hegel's students, Ludwig Feuerbach (1804–1872),[55] rejected Hegel's idealism and shifted to a materialist perspective, arguing that religion is a human creation and that materialism was the true basis of reality.[56]

Karl Marx embraced Feuerbach's materialism but criticized his focus on individual human essence rather than the broader societal structures that shape human existence.[57] Unlike Feuerbach, who saw materialism primarily as a way to understand human nature, Marx regarded it as fundamentally revolutionary—a means to challenge and dismantle not just abstract philosophical systems, religious beliefs, and theological doctrines, but also the political institutions that supported oppressive social structures.[58] Although Marx criticized both Feuerbach's anthropology

---

51. Institute for Unification, "Juche Ideology," 30.

52. Carswell, "materialism."; American Heritage, "materialistic.";

53. Cambridge University, "summary"; "The original Greek word for atheism is *atheos*, meaning 'god-forsaken' or 'impious' and 'those who are thought to be uncivilized or in some other way beyond the pale.'"

54. Notre Dame, "Review of Hegel."

55. Colin Harper, "Discovering the Truth"; Ludwig Feuerbach (1804–1872), a student of Hegel, understood that the divine essence and the human essence are really identical; religion creates a split within human beings, and the highest qualities of human nature are projected into an imaginary realm and onto an imaginary being supposed to exist apart from man. For Feuerbach, "the absolute Being, the God of man, is his own nature," and the riches which properly belong to it are squandered in being attributed to an imaginary other.

56. John G. Wright, "Feuerbach."

57. Mitias, "Marx"; Marx insisted that religion is "the opium of the people" and urged the abolition of religion, mainly Christianity. Also, Marx criticized Feuerbach's concept of men being unhistorical and abstract entity while he takes the concept of men being "ensemble of social relations" because a man is a social being.

58. Mitias, "Marx."

and Hegel's idealism, Hegel's influence on Marx remained profound. Both thinkers were united by the ultimate aim of human liberation, though they pursued it through markedly different approaches.[59]

Atheistic ideologies influenced major historical events, such as the French Revolution (1789), which sought political transformation and democratic ideals but left a legacy of mass violence and the rise of dictatorship.[60] The Russian Communist Revolution (from 1917 to 1922), grounded in the materialist theories of Marx and Engels, marked another transformative moment. Under Lenin's leadership, the Bolsheviks overthrew the existing regime and established a new order. Lenin's followers later synthesized his theories with Marx's ideas to create *Marxism-Leninism*, an ideological framework that shaped the global communist movement. This framework profoundly influenced Kim Il Sung, who later adapted its principles to develop Juche, a unique ideology that shaped the development of the North Korean regime.[61]

Internalization of Juche Ideology

According to Hiebert, we absorb our core culture during childhood and later take its principles for granted, accepting them as self-evident.[62] Murray Thomas highlights that a significant portion of North Korean school textbooks is devoted to Juche ideology, with the following approximate distribution of major themes: idolization of the Supreme Leader (40–50 percent), anti-imperialism (20–30 percent), the superiority of the North Korean communist system (15–25 percent), communist morals (5–10 percent), and anti-South Korea sentiment (5–10 percent).[63] The main goal of North Korean education is to mold citizens into individuals who are aligned with Juche principles and socialist values. Education functions as a

---

59. Balas, "Marx and Hegel." He writes, "Both philosophers examined patterns of development in human history, by which they attempted to understand modern society. Marx went further and produced a theory in accordance with these patterns of history to figure out *what needs to be done* for societies to progress. On the other hand, Hegel believes that we cannot rationally aim for an ideal like Marx's communism, as historical progress happens naturally, by itself. The inverse *dialectical* methods they use are reflected in the roles they give to philosophy."

60. Liulevicius, "Marx, Engels."

61. Resis, "Vladimir Lenin."

62 Hiebert, *Transforming Worldviews*, 90.

63. Thomas, "Democratic People's," 133–151.

means of social control, shaping personal identities and preserving political legitimacy.[64] Political socialization is further reinforced through systematic ideological education and cultural expressions, such as festivals and rituals tied to the life cycle.[65]

Jin-Man Kim observes that while the North Korean regime has long sought to manipulate the consciousness of its citizens, some studies suggest that the internal values of North Koreans increasingly diverge from those imposed by the regime.[66] This shift is influenced by social dynamics and resource distribution. Though the regime's mechanisms aim to maintain the Kim dynasty's rule, there is growing tension between official ideology and the lived experiences of the people. The internalization of Juche often involves outward conformity, but may not reflect genuine belief, with external influences and material hardships contributing to increasing ideological divergence.[67]

Juche Doctrine

It is beyond the scope of this research to examine every aspect of the Juche doctrine. However, since the essence of Christianity centers on God, humanity, and God's plan for redeeming human sin through Jesus Christ, it seems fitting to explore parallel themes within Juche: the supreme being (*Suryong*), human beings, socio-political life, and the ultimate victory (of communism).

Supreme Being

The concept of a supreme being within the Juche ideology can be understood by examining the *Ten Great Principles of the Establishment of the Unitary Ideology System* in North Korea.[68] These principles were created to fortify a system of absolute control and suppress any potential resistance to the establishment of Kim Jong Il's succession. While the Christian Ten Commandments emphasize the exclusivity of God in only the first three

---

64. Byung Ro Kim, *Internalization of Juche*, 1–7.
65. Young Sup Song, "Socio-cultural Factors," 44.
66. Jin-Man Kim, "Internalization-mechanism," 352.
67. Jin-Man Kim, "Internalization-mechanism," 353.
68. Gwang Myung Kim, "Mission Strategies," 20.

commandments, North Korea's Ten Principles prominently feature Kim Il Sung's name in every commandment, underscoring the absolutization of his authority.[69] The first five principles, in particular, focus on demanding unconditional loyalty to him:[70]

> The rules that dictate every aspect of daily life for North Koreans were initially proposed by Young Joo Kim in 1967 and later publicly introduced by Kim Jong Il in 1974.
> 1. We must use every resource we have to struggle to subsume all of society under the revolutionary philosophy of the Great Leader Kim Il Sung.
> 2. Comrade Kim Il Sung, the Great Leader, must have our complete loyalty.
> 3. Comrade Kim Il Sung, the Great Leader, must have unquestionable power.
> 4. The Great Leader Comrade Kim Il Sung's revolutionary theory must become our religion, and his instructions must become our guiding principles.
> 5. We must completely adhere to the idea of unqualified obedience when carrying out the directives of the Great Leader, comrade Kim Il Sung.

The remaining five outline the resulting behavioral principles:[71]

> 6. With a focus on the Great Leader, Comrade Kim Il Sung, we must develop the doctrine, revolutionary unity, and willpower of the entire party.
> 7. We must take a cue from the Great Leader, Comrade Kim Il Sung, and embrace the communist appearance, cutting-edge working practices, and people-centered work style.
> 8. We must honor the tremendous Leader, Comrade Kim Il Sung, for the political life he gave us and faithfully return his tremendous political trust and thoughtfulness with increased political knowledge and talent.
> 9. We must adopt strict organizational rules to ensure that the whole party, country, and military function as one under the sole and undisputed direction of Comrade Kim Il Sung, the Great Leader.

---

69. Gwang Myung Kim, "Mission Strategies," 20.
70. Gwang Myung Kim, "Mission Strategies," 22.
71. Gwang Myung Kim, "Mission Strategies," 22.

10. In order to complete the revolution started by Comrade Kim Il Sung, it must be passed down through generations.[72]

The Ten Principles were specifically drafted for Kim Il Sung and served as criteria for evaluating the words and actions of North Korean citizens.[73] Kim Il Sung's unitary ideology, centered on humanity, asserts his absolute authority in both political and social spheres, with the aim of constructing a utopian society on earth. However, from a temporal perspective, his authority is neither eternal nor directed toward an everlasting paradise. In contrast, God, as the creator of the world, holds ultimate authority and will ultimately judge it.

Human Beings

The former Supreme People's Assembly Standing Committee Chairman, Jang Yop Hwang, masterminded the contents of the Juche ideology, though its authorship is officially credited to Kim Il Sung.[74] Within this framework, Juche defines humans as the ultimate authorities, holding supreme control and decision-making power in all matters.[75] As such, Juche claims that the fundamental nature of humanity consists of three core attributes—independence (or lordship), creativity, and consciousness (or awareness)—and that these qualities elevate humans to the status of supreme and most powerful beings, enabling them to fulfill the roles of governors and rebuilders of the world.[76]

Independence, as described in Juche, refers to humanity's lordship, where all things are subordinated to serve human purposes by overcoming the constraints of nature or societal limitations.[77] This concept is regarded as essential to human existence, suggesting that without such independence, human life is meaningless, even if one is physically alive. This perspective stands in stark contrast to the Christian understanding of humanity. In Christianity, human authority is framed as stewardship over God's creation—a responsibility entrusted by God, the ultimate LORD of

---

72. "Ten Principles for the Establishment of a Monolithic Ideological System," para 7.
73. Gwang Myung Kim, "Mission Strategies," 4.
74. "Jang Yop Hwang," para 3.
75. "On the Juche Idea," para 9.
76. Jong Il Kim, *On Some Questions*, 1–8.
77. Jong Il Kim, *On Some Questions*, 3–7.

all things. Here, human lordship is exercised in submission to and under the authority of God's divine lordship.

With regard to creativity, Kim Il Sung and Kim Jong Il stated that humans, as social beings, possess creativity that enables them to reshape the world to align with the requirements and purposes of their lordship.[78] They emphasized that it is the purpose-driven nature of humanity to reform the world and chart their own destiny.[79] Concerning awareness, Kim Jong Il remarked, "Awareness is the nature of social beings, enabling them to understand both the world and themselves, thereby directing all activities toward reformation."[80]

Socio-Political Life and Salvation

Juche ideology offers a vision of eternal life through socio-political existence, separate from physical life.[81] It critiques societal structures without addressing the concept of original sin, focusing instead on political and social transformation as the means to salvation.[82] In contrast, Christianity focuses on the inherent sin in humanity, asserting that salvation requires personal transformation, not just socio-political change. Juche views revenge as a justified response to injustice, while Christianity teaches that true justice requires more than just societal change—it calls for personal repentance and transformation. Christianity sees the root cause of corruption and injustice as the inherent sinful nature of humanity, which requires divine intervention for healing and redemption.

The Final Victory in the End

Kim Il Sung first used the expression *final victory* in a telegram sent to Soviet leader Joseph Stalin two months after the start of the Korean War.[83] In the message, he stated, "We have firmly resolved to win the final victory in the struggle against the American interventionists, who are trying anew to

78. Il Sung Kim, *Foreign Reporters*, 325.
79. Jung Il Kim, *Juche Philosophy*, 11.
80. Jung Il Kim, *Juche Philosophy*, 48.
81. Byung Ro Kim, *Religiosity*, 5.
82. Gwang Myung Kim, "Mission Strategies," 38.
83. Benjamin Young, "Final Victory."

enslave Korea."[84] Since that time, the North Korean regime has continued to promote the idea that the final victory of reunification is imminent, the Korean revolution is almost finished, and the North Korean people must persist in their work in factories and fields to accomplish this objective.[85] Kim Jong Il later built upon this concept through his national development initiative to achieve *Kangsong Taeguk* (a strong and prosperous country). This project was rooted in *military-first politics*[86] and aimed to challenge capitalism and imperialism, which were portrayed as forces of evil.[87]

In examining Juche ideology—its development, internalization, and doctrinal themes—valuable insights emerge that can provide a foundation for effectively introducing the Christian truth and worldview to North Korean defectors. By reframing familiar themes such as loyalty and sacrifice, contrasting the principle of self-reliance with dependence on God, and leveraging the concept of internalization, this approach can guide defectors in internalizing the Christian faith, offering them hope and transformation. Building on an understanding of Juche ideology and its profound impact on the worldview of North Koreans, it is vital to approach conversion as a transformative journey. The following section will explore the nature of conversion and its significance within this context.

Conversion as a Process

The Hebrew term *shuv*, meaning "to turn back" or "to return," and the Greek words *epistrophe* and *metanoeo*, which mean "turning toward God," are closely related to the English concept of *conversion*.[88] In particular, *metanoeo*, along with its noun form *metanoia*, is a central term in the New Testament. Unlike its classical Greek usage, which mostly referred to a shift in thinking, *metanoia* in the New Testament signifies a transformation of the heart.[89]

Scholars have highlighted various dimensions of conversion in an effort to provide a more comprehensive understanding of the concept. For

---

84. Benjamin Young, "Final Victory."
85. Benjamin Young, "Final Victory."
86. Woo Gon Chung, "National Development," 35–66.
87. Gwang Myung Kim, "Mission Strategies," 6.
88. Bloesch, "Meaning of Conversion."
89. Bloesch, "Meaning of Conversion."

instance, Donald G. Bloesch emphasizes that conversion involves not only a personal spiritual transformation but also a shift in social attitudes:

> Even though conversion is fundamentally a change in one's relationship with God, this spiritual change entails a transformation in social attitudes as well. Conversion is primarily a spiritual event, but it has profound implications in the secular or public sphere of man's life. It points man toward a spiritual goal, but he is called to pursue this spiritual goal in the midst of the grime and agony of this world.[90]

John Wesley remained steadfast to the fundamental message of Scripture when he defined conversion as a complete transformation of the inner being and outward life, shifting from sin to holiness, a turning.[91]

Similarly, scholars such as Rambo and Farhadian emphasized the dynamic and multifaceted nature of conversion. They described it as "a process of religious change that takes place in a dynamic force field of people, events, ideologies, institutions, expectations, and experiences."[92] Although the Bible contains instances of instant conversion, Rambo emphasized that in most cases, the process is gradual and complex, influenced by a combination of individual, societal, cultural, and religious elements.[93] These forces are deeply connected to an individual's historical context, personal needs, and circumstances, all of which uniquely shape their conversion experience.[94]

Paul Hiebert underscored the need for total transformation in conversion, arguing that genuine and lasting conversion involves not only changes in behavior and faith but also profound shifts at the worldview level.[95] From these perspectives, it becomes evident that conversion is a gradual process that takes time. Furthermore, when examining the various factors and components that influence conversion, a multidisciplinary approach is more effective than narrowing the focus to a few specific factors.[96] The next section will examine the transformation of worldview as it relates to achieving a comprehensive and complete transformation.

90. Bloesch, "Meaning of Conversion."
91. "Conversion," *A Dictionary of Methodism.*
92. Rambo and Farhadian. "Converting," 24.
93. Rambo, "Psychology of Conversion," 158.
94. Rambo, *Religious Conversion*, 7–12.
95. Hiebert, *Transforming Worldviews*, 315.
96. Rambo, *Religious Conversion*, 5.

Worldview Transformation

Cultures are constantly evolving, and these cultural changes often lead to shifts in worldviews. However, worldview changes tend to occur more gradually, as they operate primarily at a subconscious level.[97] This section will explore the concept of worldview, the process of transformation, and key themes that underpin a biblical worldview.

The Concept of Worldview

Immanuel Kant was the first to introduce the term *worldview* (*Weltanschauung*), which refers to the way individuals interpret the meaning of the world and their position in it.[98] Although Kant used the term only once and did not assign it a central role in his philosophy, his assertion that reason, independent of tradition and religion, is the path to such understanding profoundly influenced the future development of worldview studies.[99] During the nineteenth century, the movements of Romanticism and Idealism gave significant importance to Weltanschauung within their philosophical frameworks. By the 1940s, educated Germans often used the term to refer to a comprehensive outlook on life and the world, ultimately establishing it as a recognized academic concept.

Paul Hiebert describes a group's worldview as the core set of beliefs—cognitive, emotional, and evaluative—that shape their understanding of reality and guide how they organize their lives.[100] Similarly, Charles Kraft describes worldview as the sum of culturally shaped images and assumptions that influence how individuals perceive and respond to reality.[101] He further emphasizes that worldview is an integral part of culture, shaping the most basic assumptions and presuppositions upon which people construct their lives. For a more holistic perspective, James Sire, in the 5th edition of *The Universe Next Door*, provides a comprehensive definition of worldview:[102]

---

97. Hiebert, *Transforming Worldviews*, 316.
98. Goheen and Bartholomew, *Crossroads*, 11–12.
99. Goheen and Bartholomew, *Crossroads*, 12–14
100. Hiebert, *Transforming Worldviews*, 25.
101. Kraft, *Christian Witness*, 12.
102. Sire, *Next Door*.

A worldview is a commitment, a fundamental orientation of the heart, that can be expressed as a story or in a set of presuppositions (assumptions which may be true or entirely false) that we hold (consciously or subconsciously, consistently or inconsistently) about the basic constitution of reality, and that provides the foundation on which we live and move and have our being.[103]

To better understand worldview, it's important to explore how shifts in worldview contribute to deeper changes in one's understanding of reality and purpose, which ultimately lead to spiritual transformation.

Transformation

God invites people to undergo spiritual transformation by returning to Him as their Creator and LORD, leaving behind all forms of idols.[104] When individuals respond to this call, they experience spiritual transformation. However, humans can only observe outward transformation through actions and words. To better understand transformation, it is helpful to analyze changes at the level of worldviews.[105] In terms of transformation within cognitive categories, the biblical perspective emphasizes relational categories.[106] This is grounded in the belief that humans, being created in God's image, are meant to exist in a relationship with him. Transformation in relational categories teaches us to develop and nurture our relationship with God over time, recognizing that breaking this relationship is understood as a sin.[107]

A true transformation involves all three dimensions of culture—cognitive, affective, and evaluative.[108] Similarly, a genuine conversion also involves all three levels of culture: "behavior and rituals, beliefs, and worldviews."[109] This means that alongside visible behavioral changes, there must also be profound, invisible shifts in underlying beliefs. Inasmuch, genuine conversion includes transformation at the worldview level.[110]

---

103. Sire, *Next Door*, 21.
104. Hiebert, *Transforming Worldviews*, 307.
105. Hiebert, *Transforming Worldviews*, 307–8.
106. Ryken, *Christian Worldview*, 51.
107. Hiebert, *Transforming Worldviews*, 309.
108. Hiebert, *Transforming Worldviews*, 312.
109. Hiebert, *Transforming Worldviews*, 316.
110. Hiebert, *Transforming Worldviews*, 315.

Without such a change, the gospel risks being distorted and subordinated to the surrounding culture.

Over time, an unchanged worldview can undermine the integrity of faith. In the context of cross-cultural witnessing, Charles Kraft advises that outsiders or missionaries should act as advocates for change rather than implementers. Imposed changes, no matter how beneficial they may seem, often remain superficial and fail to address deeper, foundational assumptions.[111] True transformation at the worldview level must be initiated and implemented by the insiders who belong to the culture in partnership with God.[112] The role of missionaries is to support and guide this process, ensuring that change takes root at the deepest levels of belief and understanding.

Having explored worldview transformation in terms of cultural dimensions and layers, the next section will delve into the biblical worldview and its core themes to better understand the ultimate goal of transformation.

Toward a Biblical Worldview

Christians are called to live godly lives that reflect their unshakable faith in the LORD Jesus Christ and a transformed worldview, even amidst pressure from various competing worldviews. The biblical account of the twelve spies sent into the Promised Land provides a striking illustration. Of the twelve, only two—Caleb and Joshua—aligned their perspective with God's plan and will, while the other ten described the land as "a land that devours its inhabitants" (Num 13:32–33). The mistaken viewpoint of the ten spies led the Israelites to complain and doubt God's will and promises. Tragically, their unbelief resulted in their downfall, as they perished in the wilderness. This account demonstrates the profound consequences of holding unbiblical worldviews, which can lead to devastating outcomes.

Because God reveals himself in the Bible, a truly biblical worldview requires seeing everything exactly as God does. However, human understanding of Scripture is inherently limited and often shaped by personal, historical, and cultural contexts. As such, rather than claiming to have fully attained a biblical worldview, believers are on a continual journey *toward* it.[113] Charles Kraft offers a valuable critique of the term "biblical worldview," warning that it could lead to the mistaken belief that God

---

111. Kraft, *Christian Witness*, 464–65.
112. Kraft, *Christian Witness*, 465.
113. Hiebert, *Transforming Worldviews*, 265.

endorses all aspects of Hebrew culture, some of which may not be considered holy.[114] According to Kraft, God uses the worldviews of the Hebrews and their prophets as a means to communicate greater truths, particularly those revealed through Hebraic history and the life and ministry of Jesus Christ. Therefore, Kraft recommends alternative terms like "Jesus' perspectives or paradigms" or "Kingdom perspectives or paradigms" to convey more accurately the Christian mindset believers should strive to adopt.[115]

It is important to understand that worldviews are deeply ingrained frameworks that evolve over time and often transcend individual interpretation. These worldviews reflect a profound continuity within the overarching biblical narrative.[116] Since no single worldview can fully capture the ultimate reality revealed in Scripture, it is essential to engage deeply with the key themes, core elements, and unity of the biblical narrative. These foundational insights help believers interpret and apply Scripture faithfully, guiding them toward a more authentic biblical worldview..

Foundational Worldview Themes in the Bible

This section explores key underlying themes of a biblical worldview. A worldview, understood as a set of foundational beliefs that shape how we perceive and interpret the world, is often categorized by theologians into four central elements: "Creation, the Fall, Grace, and Glory."[117] Additionally, Paul Hiebert identified biblical worldview themes through the lens of the three dimensions of culture. This study will integrate aspects of Hiebert's framework into the data analysis, examining these themes throughout this section.

Cognitive Worldview Themes

The following themes and counterthemes from the cognitive worldview can be found in the Old Testament and are fulfilled in the New Testament: *Creator and Creation, Revelation and Human Knowledge, Kingdom of God*

---

114. Kraft et al., *Christianity with Power*, 103.
115. Kraft et al., *Christianity with Power*, 103–4.
116. Hiebert, *Transforming Worldviews*, 265.
117. Ryken, *Christian Worldview*, 33–34.

and *Kingdom of This World*, *Organic and Mechanistic*, and *Group and Individual Themes*.[118]

When discussing the themes of *Creator and Creation*, Kraft emphasizes that God in the Bible is not only the Creator but also the Sustainer of the universe.[119] This implies that the distinction between Creator and creation in the Bible is contingent rather than ontological, emphasizing a relational rather than an essential divide.[120] Every aspect of God's ongoing creation is essential for sustaining all existence. He upholds creation through his Word, governs by his decrees, and seeks to restore and forgive creation's disobedience.[121] Humanity, having pledged allegiance to another king, Satan, is called back to God's dominion.

Regarding the *Kingdom of God and the Kingdoms of this World*, Brian J. Walsh notes, "God's kingship is covenantal in nature."[122] Though not fully realized, the kingdom of God was brought to earth through Christ, and in him, the kingdom is alive and active. While the kingdoms of this world continue to operate under human power, flawed systems, and corruption.[123] Those who receive Christ experience the power of the kingdom and a foretaste of the coming age.

On the topic of the *Organic and Mechanistic Theme*, the fundamental metaphor in Scripture is *organic*, emphasizing the interconnectedness of individuals with one another and with the broader human family.[124] In contrast, a mechanistic perspective values control, power, and self-preservation, often relying on force, manipulation, and technical strategies to maintain dominance.[125] Scripture, however, underscores relationships grounded in shalom, characterized by love and peace.[126] In essence, shalom represents the ideal state of how things are meant to be.[127] Within Christianity, this encompasses the internal dynamics of the Holy Trinity, humanity, and families. In a state of shalom, every created entity would maintain

---

118. Hiebert, *Transforming Worldviews*, 268–95.
119. Kraft, *Christian Witness*, 204.
120. Hiebert, *Transforming Worldviews*, 269.
121. Hiebert, *Transforming Worldviews*, 273.
122. Walsh and Middleton, *Transforming Vision*, 79.
123. Hiebert, *Transforming Worldviews*, 278.
124. Hiebert, *Transforming Worldviews*, 286.
125. Kavanaugh, *Following Christ*, 42.
126. Hiebert, *Transforming Worldviews*, 286.
127. Plantinga, *Not the Way*, 10,

its unique completeness and harmony while fostering numerous mutually beneficial relationships with other entities.

Regarding *group and individual themes*, the creation story in Genesis emphasizes that the only thing God declared as *bad* was Adam's solitude. When God created a woman as his partner, their relationship eventually grew into "a family, a community, and a city."[128] The Scripture teaches that, at the core of human identity, there is no distinction between others—there is only "us." Christians receive a new identity as members of God's family, an eternal identity that transcends all earthly affiliations.[129] Believers are called to join with those in need of redemption, mirroring how Jesus, the Christ, entered into our humanity to be united with us. By identifying with the impoverished and the lost, we can live out an incarnational mission, demonstrating the same mercy that God has graciously shown to each of us.

Affective Themes

Scripture presents various affective themes, exemplified in *the fruit of the Spirit*. Paul describes them as "love, joy, peace, patience, kindness, goodness, faithfulness, gentleness, and self-control" (Gal 5:22–23), all of which sharply contrasts with the sinful acts that stem from the sinful nature (Gal 5:19–21). Paul highlights the dichotomy between "two creations" and "two kingdoms." The acts of the sinful nature represent "the fallen reign of the first Adam," who surrendered his dominion to Satan, while the fruit of the Spirit reflects the rule of the "last Adam, Jesus Christ."[130] As Hiebert describes, the righteousness inherent in the fruit of the Spirit reflects the nature and character of Christ and serves as visible evidence of his transforming work, shaping believers into his likeness.[131]

The essence of *love* in the context of the Bible is "sacrifice and selflessness," as exposited in Rom 5:8, "While we were still sinners, Christ died for us."[132] This revolutionary *agape* love embodies unwavering dedication to the well-being of others, extending beyond friends to include adversaries.

---

128. Ryken, *Christian Worldview*, 55.
129. Hiebert, *Transforming Worldviews*, 289–90
130. Fesko, *The Fruit*, 56.
131. Kraft, *Christianity in Culture*, 44.
132. Fesko, *The Fruit*, 57.

It is redemptive rather than punitive, aiming to transform rather than vanquish opponents.[133]

Joy is vividly illustrated in Zeph 3:17, where God delights in his people with exuberance, celebrating them despite his full awareness of earthly injustice and sin.[134] As the source of joy, God fosters it through "good relationships with him and with others."[135] This joy is inherently other-centered, finding fulfillment in the shared joy of others. Rooted in the eschatological salvation granted by God, this joy arises from the forgiveness of sins and the foretaste of ultimate redemption, aptly termed "joy in the LORD."[136]

Peace, as emphasized in the Pauline epistles, pertains to harmonious relationships within communities, often involving the cessation of hostilities.[137] True peace is not the absence of conflict but the pursuit of justice, forgiveness, and reconciliation. Following Jesus' example, we are called to engage with our adversaries, striving for justice, extending forgiveness, and fostering reconciliation. Even when humanity loathed and rejected him, he pursued us with unwavering love. Through his crucifixion and resurrection, he opened the way to a new life, extending an invitation to his enemies to join him in a community characterized by love and mutual respect.[138]

Patience and long-suffering, especially in Pauline epistles, relate to "the passive but tenacious side of love."[139] Rom 2:4 attributes these qualities to God's response to human arrogance, while 1 Cor 13:4 describes them as core aspects of love.[140] Patience, as portrayed in Scripture, is not mere passive endurance but active submission to the guidance of the Holy Spirit. It counteracts behaviors such as "outbursts of rage" (Gal 5:20) and "provoking one another" (Gal 5:26), fostering unity and understanding.[141] Patience and long-suffering are "the antidote to 'outbursts of rage' (Gal 5:20) or 'provoking one another' (Gal 5:26)."[142]

---

133. Hiebert, *Transforming Worldviews*, 292.
134. Pickett, *Cultivating the Gifts*, 123.
135. Hiebert, *Transforming Worldviews*, 294.
136. Fee, *Paul*, 118.
137. Fee, *Paul*, 119.
138. Hiebert, *Transforming Worldviews*, 294.
139. Hiebert, *Transforming Worldviews*, 294
140. Fee, *Paul, the Spirit*, 119.
141. Hiebert, *Transforming Worldviews*, 295.
142. Fee, *Paul*, 120.

Precedent and Related Literature

Evaluative Themes

The guiding principles for addressing biblical ethical issues are rooted in God's holiness and righteousness.[143] To fully grasp the theme of *good versus evil*, it is essential first to understand the biblical concept of *holiness*. In the Bible, *holy* is defined as "set apart for God, consecrated, and dedicated to him." Holiness encompasses both dedication and the process of becoming like God, through imitation and conformity to his character. Therefore, in the Bible, good is defined not by our short-term comfort, but by what honors God, fulfills his will, and aligns with his nature, prioritizing our long-term well-being over temporary ease.[144] Similarly, sin is not merely the violation of impersonal rules; rather, it is a severance of relationships with God and others.[145] Evil, as Paul explains in Romans 8, encompasses the corruption and decay that all of creation has endured as a result of human sin. Creation exists in a state of bondage, yearning for liberation and redemption. This suggests that much of what we perceive as natural evil may ultimately stem from humanity's sin.[146] Righteousness, as described by Millard Erickson, is a manifestation of God's holiness that governs his relationship with creation. While holiness reflects God's absolute moral purity and separation from sin, righteousness is the active expression of that holiness through his just, fair, and morally upright actions.[147]

Regarding the theme of *justification and restoration*, the Apostle Paul writes, "If anyone is in Christ, he is a new creation; the old has gone, the new has come" (2 Cor 5:17). While holiness is not something humans can achieve on their own, it is fundamental to the new nature and God-given mode of existence in Christ.[148] In the New Testament, salvation is presented as both individual and corporate. Salvation is corporate because God is forming a new community, uniting believers into one body that works together to serve and edify the whole. In addition, humanity is called to exercise dominion over the material creation for its restoration—a dominion characterized by humble service, modeled by Christ himself.[149]

---

143. Hiebert, *Transforming Worldviews*, 295.
144. Packer, *Rediscovering*, 19.
145. Hiebert, *Transforming Worldviews*, 296.
146. Erickson, *Christian Theology*, 452.
147. Erickson, *Christian Theology*, 313–14.
148. Hiebert, *Transforming Worldviews*, 299.
149. Burket and Hill, s. v. "creation."

Thus far, key biblical worldview themes have been identified across all three dimensions of this study. The next section will outline the research methodology employed in this investigation.

Literature on Research Methodology

This section examines qualitative research methodology and Grounded Theory, highlighting their principles, applications, and significance to the study.

Qualitative Research Methodology

Qualitative research involves exploring and interpreting data without the use of statistical methods or numerical measurement. According to Strauss and Corbin, qualitative research is ideal for fieldwork-based studies that interpret individuals' experiences, particularly in complex areas like chronic illness. It is useful for both emerging and well-established topics, especially when exploring abstract phenomena like emotions that are challenging to quantify. They outline three key components: data collection from various sources such as interviews, systematic data analysis, and dissemination through verbal or written reports.[150]

Considering the study aims to gain a more profound insight into people's lived experiences, a qualitative research methodology will be adopted. While there are various approaches to conducting qualitative research, this section will focus specifically on Grounded Theory methodology, as it provides the framework through which this research aims to develop a theory.

Grounded Theory Research Methodology

The Grounded Theory technique was originally developed by sociologists Barney Glaser and Anselm Strauss.[151] Strauss and Corbin define Grounded Theory as "theory that was derived from data, systematically gathered and analyzed through the research process."[152] This approach ensures that the resulting theory remains closely aligned with reality, as it emerges

---

150. Strauss and Corbin, *Basics*, 10–12.
151. Strauss and Corbin, *Basics*, 9.
152. Strauss and Corbin, *Basics*, 12.

organically from the data rather than being influenced by preconceived notions or theories held by the researcher.[153] Furthermore, Grounded Theory is described as "both science and art," requiring researchers to strike a careful balance between the systematic rigor of scientific methods and the creative interpretation necessary for meaningful analysis throughout the research process:

> It is science in the sense of maintaining a certain degree of rigor and grounding analysis in data. Creativity manifests itself in the ability of researchers to aptly name categories, ask stimulating questions, make comparisons, and extract an innovative, integrated, realistic scheme from masses of unorganized raw data.[154]

The creative aspect of Grounded Theory has historically been overshadowed by the emphasis on objectivity, a trend that has similarly affected qualitative research. However, Charmaz contends that using Grounded Theory in a contemporary, reflective approach enables ongoing interaction with the data, fostering the creation of new idea.[155] This approach not only aids in conceptual analysis but also allows researchers to capture their evolving ideas and important questions throughout the research process. By embracing this dynamic and adaptive exploration of the data, Grounded Theory methodologies provide a framework for capturing researchers' fleeting insights and addressing pressing inquiries as they arise, ensuring a rich and nuanced analysis.[156]

To effectively engage with Grounded Theory methodology, understanding the following concepts is crucial. First, *coding* involves "extracting concepts from raw data and developing them in terms of their properties and dimensions." Second, *concepts* are classified into various levels: "Lower-level concepts to high-level concepts." High-level concepts are referred to as *categories* or *themes*, which represent the overarching ideas inferred from a group of lower-level concepts.[157] *Property* is the attributes that shape and characterize concepts, while *dimension* refers to the differences within properties that help define the scope and specificity of a concept. Third, *constant comparisons* involve the analytical process of examining different pieces of data to identify their similarities and differences. This process is

153. Corbin and Strauss, *Qualitative Research 3e*, 12.
154. Corbin and Strauss, *Qualitative Research 2e*, 13.
155. Charmaz, *Grounded Theory*, 179.
156. Charmaz, *Grounded Theory*, 179.
157. Corbin and Strauss, *Qualitative Research 3e*, 159–160.

vital for separating different categories and themes and for identifying the unique properties and dimensions of each. Fourth, *theoretical sampling* involves selecting samples based on concepts that emerge from the data.[158] The objective of theoretical sampling is to investigate specific locations, individuals, or events that provide the best opportunities to identify variations within concepts and to enhance categories by exploring their properties and dimensions more thoroughly.[159] Fifth, *saturation* occurs when a category is "saturated," meaning "no new information emerges during coding, and no additional properties, dimensions, conditions, actions/interactions, or consequences are identified in the data."[160]

Strauss and Corbin, along with Charmaz, outline a systematic approach to coding in qualitative research, dividing it into several stages. The first stage, known as *open coding* or *initial coding*, involves breaking down the data and identifying concepts to represent distinct elements of the raw data. During this process, concepts are also defined with respect to their properties and dimensions.[161] Charmaz introduces various methods for coding, including *word-by-word coding, line-by-line coding, incident-to-incident coding*, and *in vivo* coding.[162] *In vivo* coding specifically utilizes the participants' language to develop codes.[163] A key focus at this stage is *conceptualizing*—assigning a name or label to an event that reflects its context, including the conditions or circumstances in which it occurs.[164] These labels are not arbitrary; they result from careful and thorough data analysis. Grouping concepts into categories helps researchers manage the data more effectively. These categories, often referred to as "phenomena," are powerful tools for analysis.[165]

The next stage of coding is called *axial coding*. This process involves linking subcategories to categories based on their attributes and dimensions. Unlike descriptive coding, axial coding is more conceptual. Subcategories do not focus directly on the phenomenon itself; instead, they address questions such as "when," "where," "why," "who," "how," and "with

---

158. Corbin and Strauss, *Qualitative Research 3e*, 65, 73, 159,.
159. Strauss and Corbin, *Basics*, 201.
160. Strauss and Corbin, *Basics*, 136.
161. Corbin and Strauss, *Qualitative Research 3e*, 195.
162. Charmaz, *Grounded Theory*, 50–55.
163. Charmaz, *Grounded Theory*, 55.
164. Straus and Corbin, *Basics*, 110.
165. Straus and Corbin, *Basics*, 113–14.

what consequences" related to the phenomenon. This approach enhances the concept's explanatory depth and analytical power.[166]

Following axial coding, the next stage is *selective coding*. This involves refining and integrating the theory[167] by exploring the relationships among the substantive codes and incorporating them into a theory.[168] The initial step in this integration process is identifying the "central or core category" into which all other categories can be included.[169] Writing a storyline can help identify this core category and support the connection of concepts.[170] Additional methods, such as revisiting memos or using visual tools like graphics, can further support this integration. In the end, researchers refine the theory by eliminating unnecessary elements and addressing gaps in underdeveloped categories.[171]

Charmaz critiques the rigid coding standards of Straussian Grounded Theory, advocating for a more flexible approach that encourages creative interaction with data. She emphasizes the importance of maintaining a tolerance for ambiguity and openness to the emergence of new categories and techniques during the research process.[172]

Summary

Chapter Two has explored the identities of North Korean defectors and the Juche ideology, which reflects their worldview. It also discussed the concept of worldviews in general, the idea of conversion, and key themes related to a biblical worldview. Furthermore, a brief introduction to the Grounded Theory methodology was included. The next chapter delves into the research approach that will be employed in this study.

---

166. Straus and Corbin, *Basics*, 124–25.
167. Straus and Corbin, *Basics*, 143.
168. Charmaz, *Grounded Theory*, 63.
169. Straus and Corbin, *Basics*, 146.
170. Straus and Corbin, *Basics*, 148.
171. Corbin and Strauss, *Qualitative Research 3e,* 114–115.
172. Kenny and Fourie, "Contrasting," 10–11.

3

Research Methodology

THIS STUDY AIMS TO formulate a theory that elucidates the factors and processes influencing the worldview transformation of North Korean defector Christians living in South Korea. To accomplish this, the researcher has adopted a qualitative research approach, specifically Grounded Theory. Creswell emphasizes the appropriateness of qualitative methods when a detailed understanding of complex phenomena is necessary, particularly in uncovering the contextual subtleties of participants' experiences.[1] Additionally, as discussed in the previous chapter, Grounded Theory is an effective methodology for developing a theory based on data, making it a suitable choice for this study.[2]

To gain a comprehensive understanding of qualitative approaches and the Grounded Theory methodology, the researcher initially consulted John W. Creswell's *Qualitative Inquiry and Research Design*. For deeper insights into data analysis and the application of Grounded Theory, second and third editions of Strauss and Corbin's *Basics of Qualitative Research: Techniques and Procedures for Developing Grounded Theory* were referenced. Additionally, Kathy Charmaz's *Constructing Grounded Theory* was invaluable for its "less structured and more adaptable" approach.[3] Another key resource, Chang Sup Kang's *Transforming Research Methodology for Missiology: Practical Guide through Grounded Theory*, provided practical and comprehensive guidance. This work addressed a range of potential questions that

1. Creswell, *Qualitative Inquiry*, 39–40.
2. Strauss and Corbin, *Basics*, 12.
3. Creswell and Poth, *Qualitative Inquiry*, 89.

could arise during the analysis process, making it an indispensable tool for this research.

This research will employ one-on-one interviews to investigate the factors and processes involved in the worldview transformation of North Korean defectors. The study will examine their initial conversion experiences, the challenges they faced, and the specific events that contributed to their transition toward a biblical worldview. By exploring these dimensions, the research aims to construct a theory that narrates the process of their worldview transformation, identifying the key factors and stages involved. Grounded Theory methodology, with its inductive analytical approach, is particularly suited to this study, as it enables the development of theories in areas where existing research is limited. This chapter will outline the researched population, data collection methods, sampling and interview procedures, data analysis strategies, and measures to ensure validity and reliability.

Population (Participants)

Twenty North Korean defector Christians residing in South Korea have participated in this study. They were recommended by their authorities or fellow ministers, as they were believed to have undergone a significant transformation toward a biblical worldview. While specific details about their age or the locations of their conversions are not provided, the participants are geographically dispersed across South Korea, from Seoul to Jeju Island. Their roles and activities vary, including attending college, studying in theological schools, working for service organizations, serving in mission offices, and leading North Korean defector churches, either independently or as part of a North Korean ministry within a South Korean church.

Data Collection

The data for this study was gathered from a variety of sources. Literature research was primarily supported by the library of Torch Trinity Graduate University, which provided access to books, journals, theses, and electronic resources such as ProQuest. Additional materials included e-books and books from online archives and bookstores, articles and journals from the Internet, materials from symposiums, and data from the North Korean

Information Portal of the Ministry of Unification (www.nkifo.unikorea.go.kr).

For interview data collection, the researcher leveraged relationships formed while working with various North Korean ministries from 2007 to 2014. These connections facilitated meaningful interactions with North Korean defector leaders and South Korean ministers. Through these relationships, six participants were ultimately recommended by North Korean defector leaders, and eighteen participants were recommended by South Korean church pastors. The snowball sampling technique was used in the recommendation process. To facilitate the participant selection process, the researcher shared the Research Plan, approved by the Institutional Review Board (IRB), with the recommenders. The recommenders identified potential participants based on the criteria and standards outlined in the plan. Additionally, the researcher shared emerging concepts and themes from earlier interviews, enabling the recommenders to consider individuals who could provide deeper insights and contribute to the study's exploration of the research topic.

Initially, the researcher relied on the discretion of the recommenders to identify suitable participants. However, it became necessary to exclude four individuals from the study—one recommended by a defector leader and three recommended by South Korean ministers. This decision was based on the realization that these individuals lacked the depth of transformative experiences required to enrich the emerging concepts being investigated.

Sampling and Interview Procedure

The participants were initially contacted by the recommenders to confirm their willingness to participate in an interview. Once they agreed, the researcher followed up to schedule a convenient time for the interview. In an empirical study like this, in-depth participant interviews are the primary and most critical tool, forming the foundation of the research. The researcher's active involvement in the interviews was essential to foster cooperation and ensure that the participants' stories and experiences were fully understood and analyzed for their essence and meaning.

Before conducting the official interviews, the researcher conducted pilot interviews with two defector ministers who were close friends. These pilot interviews helped identify significant concepts related to their experiences of worldview transformation. During these sessions, the researcher observed that, without clear guidance, participants tended to focus excessively on specific issues, making it challenging to collect balanced information about their transformation experiences within the time constraints. Although the researcher allowed flexibility during the actual interviews, participants were generally given a time frame of one to one and a half hours.

To address this challenge, the researcher concluded that a minimal structure was necessary to utilize the interview time effectively. This approach ensured the collection of comprehensive data about both the factors influencing and the processes involved in the participants' worldview transformations. To achieve this, the researcher asked the following six questions:

1. What was your life like before you came to Christ?
2. What were your motives for converting to Christianity?
3. In what ways did your life change after your conversion?
4. What areas of your life have you found challenging to transform since your conversion?
5. How did you overcome these difficulties?
6. How did the transformation of your worldview into a Christian perspective occur?

The participants agreed to take part in the interviews after reviewing an explanation of the research, *Study on the Worldview Transformation of North Korean Defector Christians in South Korea*, which had been approved by the Institutional Review Board.[4] They indicated their consent by signing a consent form. To comply with the Institutional Review Board's guidelines and the participants' preferences, each participant was assigned a coded name to ensure anonymity. For instance, the code name *DF* represents the fourth participant, where D corresponds to the fourth letter of the alphabet, and F indicates that the participant is female.

The participants were asked prepared open-ended questions about their worldview, focusing on significant moments of transformation from their lives prior to conversion to the present. Each interview lasted over an hour.[5] The researcher made a concerted effort to listen attentively to the

---

4. Approval number issued by Korea National Institute for Bioethics Policy: P01–201807-22-004.

5. When the depth of the interview content required further clarification, the

participants' inner voices, taking detailed memos not only on their verbal and non-verbal expressions but also on additional insights gained from various sources. This included information provided by the individuals who introduced them, conversations during shared meals, observations of their testimonies on YouTube, and attendance at Sunday worship services at their churches. Together, these efforts enhanced the clarity and validity of the researcher's understanding of the participants' data.

Initially, each participant was scheduled for a single interview. However, as the analysis progressed and significant concepts began to emerge, the researcher occasionally needed to follow up with participants by phone to gather additional data or clarify information provided during the initial interview. In one case, a second phone interview was required with a participant who had disregarded the researcher's time and narrative guidelines during the initial session. The researcher had to pause the interview mid-story due to scheduling constraints, necessitating a follow-up to complete the discussion.

Theoretical sampling, though a crucial strategy in Grounded Theory methodology, sometimes proved challenging due to its emphasis on variability and the difficulty of planning and reporting in advance—an issue that occasionally conflicted with Institutional Review Board requirements. During the sampling process, the researcher carefully identified key concepts related to each participant's worldview transformation during the interviews. To select subsequent participants who could further elaborate on emerging concepts, the researcher initially relied on information provided by the leaders who recommended potential participants. This process was supplemented by phone conversations and casual meetings with potential participants, often facilitated by the recommenders. Toward the conclusion of the interview process, theoretical saturation became evident. No new concepts emerged, and the major concepts already developed were well-understood and thoroughly substantiated by the data collected.

Data Analysis and Its Process

All interview recordings were transcribed in Korean, along with detailed memos. Any additional data collected during follow-up phone interviews was appended to the respective participant's interview file, with the interview date clearly noted. Only the portions relevant to presenting the results

---

researcher reached out to some participants via phone for additional discussions.

of this research were translated into English by the researcher. Each interview file was thoroughly reviewed, and the researcher began conceptualizing and coding using gerund forms to capture actions and behaviors. This approach, as suggested by Charmaz for the open coding stage, preserved the fluid and dynamic nature of the participants' experiences.[6]

Comparing the emerging transformation incidents with previously conceptualized or coded incidents allowed the researcher to identify their properties. Whether at the micro or macro level, this constant comparison method, as suggested by Strauss and Corbin, proved invaluable in identifying variations, raising questions, and uncovering properties and dimensions. This method was applied consistently throughout the analysis process.[7] Additionally, the researcher created memos during the analysis, capturing specific details about the participants, the essence of each interview, emerging questions, ideas, and findings. These memos supported the development of categories and facilitated constant comparisons among them. Table 5 illustrates the memos created for the participants.

After developing all the codes, the researcher proceeded with focused coding, following Charmaz's guidance to use the most important and/or commonly occurring initial codes to sort through extensive data and determine which codes best organize and analyze the information thoroughly and effectively.[8] For instance, in discussing the challenges participants faced during their worldview transformation, one participant expressed her dislike for frequent church meetings, comparing them to the compulsory meetings they were forced to attend by the North Korean regime. Participants also described struggles such as ingrained preconceptions and cultural habits from North Korea, a tendency to enforce blind obedience stemming from North Korea's idolization practices, the pursuit of utopian ideals, and an emphasis on self-accomplishment and humanism rooted in Juche ideology. These are grouped under the category "The Residual Effects of the North Korean System." The remaining categories are developed using the same systematic approach.

6. Charmaz, *Grounded Theory*, 49.

7. Strauss and Corbin, *Basics*, 67.

8. Charmaz, *Grounded Theory*, 57. While Strauss and Corbin proposed a structured framework using conditions, actions/interactions, and consequences to visualize these links, the researcher opted to develop subcategories under each category, illustrating the connections based on insights derived directly from the empirical data, in alignment with Charmaz's approach.

Table 5. An Example of Memos: Check Points/Questions Raised on the Interview Data

Code Name	Check Point(s)	Memo
HM	1) Self-Accomplishment 2) Transformation Level	He seemed to have a clear understanding of the Bible when the Holy Spirit miraculously opened up the Bible to him for 14 days in China. He was even able to win the debates with the heresy group in China. (He is an elite defector with a doctorate). However, his only focus seemed to be on how *I* could change North Korea by just remaining at the level of intellectual transformation only with a very strong determination for the work, even risking their life, without any sign of rest that comes when God plays the leadership role in his life . . . This is a sign of self-accomplishment. I remember that OM said something similar to this.
OM	1) Initial Conception of God	OM said that the NK regime only cared about its reputation because the people who complained against the regime were executed, but they didn't care about the violence and stealing happening among the people. That was why people's lives became harder, and the law of the fittest ruled. After reading the Bible the very first time, the first thing that came to his mind was, "If North Korean people accepted the system of God's kingdom, it could become a wonderful society." Then, he said, "I first received the God of this concept, not the personal God."
	2) Motives of Defectors' Ministry	He also pointed out that the North Korean people's desperation is caused by the thought that they must go and help the miserable and suffering people in the North, even risking their lives. Additionally, he told me to look into this issue for my worldview study.
	3) Self-Accomplishment/ Self-Righteousness	He was imprisoned for helping the defectors, and the only thing that held him for his 10 years of imprisonment was the belief that he did the right thing. However, toward the end of his imprisonment, he painfully realized that he was not the one (self-accomplishment) but God, who was the One who worked to establish his kingdom and kingship in the North. At that time, all OM needed was to find the only one and true God and yield to his will, delivered from the bondage of self-accomplishment.

The focused coding process was followed by axial coding, as Charmaz recommended. Axial coding reassembles the data that was fragmented during open coding, establishing relationships between categories and subcategories while defining "the properties and dimensions of a category" to provide coherence to the emerging analysis.[9] While Strauss and Corbin proposed a structured framework using conditions, actions/interactions, and consequences to visualize these links,[10] the researcher opted to develop subcategories under each category, illustrating the connections based on insights derived directly from the empirical data, in alignment with Charmaz's approach.[11]

During this process, the researcher created organizational tables to evaluate potential major categories and themes, ensuring their relevance and clarifying the relationships among them. Furthermore, as the researcher applied line-by-line coding to increase code density and identify the key factors and concepts underlying the participants' worldview transformation, a common dynamic began to emerge. This dynamic revealed that the participants consistently expressed recurring thematic concepts about God. Through careful observation of this phenomenon, the researcher identified a theme titled *Internalization of God's Word*. Refer to Screenshot 1 for the dynamics among the participants. Subsequently, all these findings were organized and analyzed using NVivo 12.

Screenshot 1. Analysis Memos on Participants Using Microsoft Word

PARTICIPANT #2
1) Obedience: !!! Gaining Conception about God-→ internalization -→ Experiencing God
    (1) Obeying the teaching to pray for even the little things everyday.
    (2) Tithing in the midst of lacking and despite of criticism

2) God answers it
    (1) God answers
    (2) God rewards her faith by giving the money back in His own says:
        -God opening a way to register at an institute to become a nurse

Comment:
1) Her strength is in experiencing God answering her prayers (12 times mentioned)
2) By trusting God in her tithing and thanksgiving offering, she experienced God who rewarded her faith by giving her back the same amount of money. Also, even though it was impossible to go to school due to lack of finance, God opened a way for her to study to become a nurse.

PARTICIPANT #19
Comment
1) Experiencing God bringing sin to light (7 times mentioned):
    mostly criticism, self-accomplishment and self-righteousness
2) Experiencing God's Word being actualized in her life through persevering prayers
3) Choosing to obey to overcome suicidal impulse

9. Charmaz, *Grounded Theory*, 60.
10. Strauss and Corbin, *Basics*, 199.
11. Charmaz, *Grounded Theory*, 61.

The constant comparison method was also employed during axial coding to compare themes and categories. This iterative process was essential to facilitate the emergence of the core concept and the development of a theory. The categories were organized and presented in tables, while various comparisons among categories were illustrated using diagrams, as detailed in Chapter 4.

During the selective coding process, the integration and refinement of the theory focused on identifying a core concept or theme with strong explanatory power. This core concept is needed to effectively capture the theoretical purpose of the research and serve as the central organizing framework that links and unifies all the categories. To facilitate the integration of the categories, the researcher utilized charts, tables, figures, and a storyline to explain the relationships between categories and the integration process. These tools provided a comprehensive view of the worldview transformation of North Korean defectors, emphasizing both its factors and processes. Additionally, a paradigm model was employed to summarize the storyline and provide a structured representation of the findings. This process of theoretical integration is a critical step in Grounded Theory methodology for building a cohesive and well-supported theory. Concluding the analysis, the researcher presented the resulting theory on the worldview transformation of North Korean defectors living in South Korea.

Validity and Reliability

Nahid Golafshani stated that "reliability and validity are conceptualized as trustworthiness, rigor, and quality in qualitative paradigm."[12] In qualitative research, *validity* refers to:

> Appropriateness of the tools, processes, and data. Whether the research question is valid for the desired outcome, the choice of methodology is appropriate for answering the research question, the design is valid for the methodology, the sampling and data analysis are appropriate, and finally, the results and conclusions are valid for the sample and context.[13]

In qualitative research, *reliability* refers to the consistency of data and findings, ensuring that the data collected and the research process yield

---

12. Golafshani, "Reliability," 597–607.
13. Leung, "Validity."

stable results across similar contexts, even when the findings are rich and diverse. It also involves maintaining consistency in responses across different data coders. Methods to enhance *reliability* include constant comparison, triangulation, and comprehensive data analysis.[14]

The researcher shared Chapters 3 and 4 of the research paper, which details the findings, with a professional who holds a PhD earned using the same methodology. The professional reviewed the coding for accuracy based on the information provided by the interview participants. He also evaluated the reliability of applying the Grounded Theory methodology to the research problem and the analysis, offering positive affirmation of the work. Additionally, the researcher reached out to five key participants to validate the accuracy of the coding and themes derived from their stories. All five participants confirmed their accuracy and expressed their positive affirmation of the work.

---

14. Silverman, "Validity, Reliability, and Generalizability," *PubMed Central*.

4

Findings

THIS RESEARCH AIMS TO construct a theory that explains the factors and processes involved in the transformation of North Korean defector Christians' worldview into a biblical one, utilizing a Grounded Theory research methodology. First, data was gathered through interviews with 20 North Korean defector Christians who journeyed through transit countries before ultimately settling in South Korea. Second, the constant comparative method was used to analyze, codify, and categorize the interview data, identifying the processes and factors contributing to their worldview transformation. Finally, based on this analysis, a theory is presented at the conclusion of this chapter to elucidate the findings. This chapter provides a detailed account of the research process, highlighting the journey from data collection to the development of a theory that explains the complex transformation of these individuals' worldviews.

Overview of Demographic Elements

The 20 participants provided the following demographic information, summarized in Table 6.

Findings

Table 6. Demographic Profile of Interview Participants

Characteristics	Participants (n=20)	Characteristics	Participants (n=20)
The Year of Defection		*Gender*	
2010–2019	4	Male	6
2000–2009	8	Female	14
1990–1999	8	*Age*	
		20–39	3
		40–49	7
		50–59	7
		60–79	3
Years of Residency in South Korea		*Duration of Christian Life*	
1–5	2	1–5 Years	2
6–10	6	6–10 Years	2
11–15	4	16–20 Years	5
16–20	6	21–25 Years	5
21–25	2	21–25 Years	6

In addition, thirteen participants are currently active in ministry; one is a writer, two are employed by service organizations, and four are university students.

Life Prior to Conversion

The information was gathered and analyzed from responses to the first question in the questionnaire: "What was your life like before you came to Christ?" This question involves examining the core values, purposes, goals, and standards of life before their conversion. Axial coding identified 128 references mentioned in the interviews, which were categorized into four main themes: Attitude toward the North Korean Regime, The Way of Life under the Regime, Life's Goals and Values under the Regime, and Resulting Challenges. Table 7 provides a summary of the interview results, organized into themes and subthemes. It also includes the number of participants who addressed each theme and subtheme, as well as the number of comments made to each.

Table 7. Themes and Subthemes of Life Prior to Conversion
(P: number of participants; C: number of comments)

Category	Themes and Subthemes	P	C
Life Prior to Conversion	*Attitude toward the Regime*	10	14
	Disillusionment with the Supreme Leader	6	6
	Resentment and Desire for Retribution toward the Party	5	8
	Hypocritical Compliance with the Regime	1	1
	The Way of Life under the Regime	14	30
	Enforcement of Absolute Loyalty to the Supreme Leader	9	17
	Indoctrination to remain loyal to the Party	8	16
	Struggles to comply with forced obedience	2	2
	Enjoyment of the privileges granted to elite class	1	1
	Uncertainty within the Rigid Social Hierarchy	7	13
	Systematic oppression	4	7
	Existential questions beyond Juche ideology	3	4
	Individualistic pursuits for personal gain	1	1
	Life experiences in concentration camps	1	1
	Life's Goals and Values under the Regime	10	26
	Aspirations for Money, Freedom, Knowledge, etc.	9	18
	Upholding Personal Values (Conscience, Sincerity, etc.)	5	8
	Resulting Challenges	15	77
	Trauma and Crisis-Induced Challenges	15	57
	Enduring hopelessness	9	18
	Persistent feelings of powerlessness	8	19
	Erosion of human dignity	6	15
	Struggles with meaninglessness and low self-worth	5	11
	Uprootedness and dependence on relatives	4	6
	Struggles with identity crisis	4	4
	Extreme loneliness	1	3
	Severe malnutrition from betrayal and persecution	1	1
	Mental and Emotional Struggles	10	24
	Emotional indicators of depression	8	17
	Heightened insecurity and anxiety	6	7
	Struggles with low confidence	3	4
	Interpersonal Struggles	5	8

FINDINGS

Attitude toward the North Korean Regime

Ten of the 20 participants provided 14 comments reflecting their attitudes toward the North Korean regime, highlighting its profoundly negative impact on their lives. Under the theme of Attitude toward the North Korean Regime, three subthemes emerged: Disillusionment with the Supreme Leader, Resentment and Desire for Retribution toward the Party, and Hypocritical Compliance with the Regime. These subthemes capture the range of emotions and coping mechanisms expressed by the participants regarding their experiences under the regime.

Disillusionment with the Supreme Leader

Six participants expressed disillusionment with the regime. One interviewee, identified as GF, explained that her disillusionment stemmed from witnessing the devastating starvation and widespread death in North Korea. She also highlighted the stark contrast between the regime's propaganda about life in South Korea and the actual wealth and freedom enjoyed there, which further deepened her disillusionment:

> Kim said that he would be with us forever, but he died. How can a god die? Secondly, we were taught that North Korea was the wealthiest country in the world. I believed it because I never had a chance to see other parts of the world. However, I started seeing corpses stacking up in the streets and in my neighborhood ... Before the *Arduous March* in North Korea, I watched the Gwangju 5.18 incident live on TV and was shocked by the clothes South Korean people were wearing ... It was interesting. Many changes took place in the minds of North Korean people, seeing the freedom that South Koreans had—even to riot ... When the *Arduous March* began ... my father went to China and brought back rice and clothes to sell in the black market, which was quite different from the communist theories ... I relinquished the reverence for Kim Il Sung [in my heart] and started longing for freedom.[1]

Two participants, DM and HM, who had the opportunity to closely observe Kim Jong Il's life due to their high-ranking positions in the government, expressed that they found no hope in the regime:

---

1. GF, Transcript, 1.

> When people were dying, Kim Jong Il did nothing but hold parties with women every night. I knew this because I held a high position in the Party. I thought to myself, 'Is this what I devoted my life to reformation for?' The instructions from Kim were clear: 'We can institute reforms only with three million Party members.' He considered the rest of the people useless to him. 'Was my commitment to reformation all for his benefit?'[2]
>
> Originally, my 'undesirable' family background prevented me from attending university. However, I was eventually recognized by Kim Jong Il and recommended by my seniors for my excellent academic performance. This led to my promotion to a position that allowed me to interact with him personally. Over time, I witnessed numerous wrongdoings and ultimately decided to adopt an anti-establishment stance against the regime.[3]

Participant IM had spent his entire life searching for the right worldview to which he could fully commit himself. However, his journey was fraught with challenges, as his highly educated and once-respected father was sent to a labor concentration camp because he spoke about freedom. With no one left to guide him, IM turned to the only resources available in North Korea—books on communist ideologies, including Juche. He delved deeply into these ideologies, studying extensively on two main topics, aiming to equip himself to live in alignment with their principles. Despite his efforts, a turning point came when his father, a secret Christian, shared a prophetic insight about the regime's future. His father exposed the regime's false and hollow foundations and ideals, which deeply challenged IM's beliefs. Struck by this revelation, he abandoned the 30 years he had devoted to Juche ideology and retreated to a remote mountain. There, he began preparing himself for the impending national disaster his father had prophesied—a disaster that would later manifest as the *Arduous March*. On the surface, his father had provided him with the following instructions:

> My father said, 'Juche is a system that turns you into a slave!' His words hit me like a thunderbolt, as if heaven and earth had been turned upside down. At that moment, the falsity of the system became clear to me, and I found myself yielding to my father's insight. He went on to reveal that the true founder of Juche was not Kim Il Sung but Jang Yop Hwang, the former chancellor of Kim Il

---

2. DM, Transcript, 2.
3. HM, Transcript, 1–2.

Sung University, from which my father had graduated. With that revelation, every shred of trust I had in the system crumbled.[4]

Resentment and Desire for Retribution toward the Party

Five individuals shared eight accounts reflecting their resentful and revengeful attitudes toward the regime. Two participants specifically described the mistreatment they endured due to their low status within North Korea's rigid social stratification system. One of them came from a Christian heritage, while the other, JF, whose father was a Korean War POW, recounted her situation. Her words are: "I was the daughter of a Korean War POW, and I harbored deep hatred toward the regime, grinding my teeth in resentment. Filled with anger and loathing, I lived in silent submission under its oppressive rule."[5]

Two participants were once deeply committed to the regime. However, upon realizing they had been deceived, their attitudes shifted drastically. One participant, OM, even considered retaliation against the regime, stating: "I was struggling and finally realized that I was deceived. From then on, hatred became the purpose of my life . . . I was once devoted to the regime as a slave . . . even without knowing it. The feeling of betrayal was great. Kim was the one who exploited my life [our lives], and I resolved that I would one day revenge . . . However, at that time, I was just struggling to survive . . . 'Once I save some money, I will do it.'"[6]

Hypocritical Compliance with the Regime

Participant JF, whose father was a Korean War POW and whose mother's family was labeled as rebellious against the regime, found a way to survive by pretending to be loyal to the regime. She recounted: "I really wanted to study. But when I found out I couldn't go to college, I felt like I was going crazy because I couldn't dream about my future anymore. This was when I was 17 years old. I was living in a completely different world from other

---

4. IM, Transcript, 13.
5. JF, Transcript, 1.
6. OM, Transcript, 1.

North Korean people. Outwardly, I acted loyal to the regime, but inwardly, I harbored rebellion in my mind."[7]

Overall, half of the participants expressed d disillusionment in Kim Jong Il, the Supreme Leader. Those who had once been deeply loyal to the regime and placed complete trust in it voiced greater disappointment than others. Additionally, participants who faced severe discrimination due to their unfavorable family backgrounds were especially eager to express their pain, citing the systematic oppression and mistreatment they endured under the regime.

The Way of Life under the Regime

Fourteen participants made 30 references to the theme of The Way of Life Under the Regime. This theme is divided into two subthemes: Enforced Absolute Loyalty to the Supreme Leader and Uncertainty within the Rigid Social Hierarchy.

Enforcement of Absolute Loyalty to the Supreme Leader

Nine participants made 17 references to the regime's enforcement of absolute loyalty toward North Korea's Supreme Leader (i.e., the Kim family). These references have been further categorized into indoctrination to remain loyal to the Party, struggles to comply with forced obedience, and enjoyment of the exclusive privileges granted to the elite class.

Indoctrination to Remain Loyal to the Party

Eight of the nine participants spoke about their indoctrinated loyalty to the Party. Participants KF, RF, and LF described their experiences as follows:

> We were extremely brainwashed. I was more loyal than other people . . . I truly believed I was the master of my life and that Kim Il Sung was a god. When we call something 'truth,' it is worth risking my life for. I thought giving my life to Kim Il Sung was worth it.[8]

---

7. JF, Transcript, 5.
8. KF, Transcript, 1.

FINDINGS

> I was fully immersed in Juche, down to my very bones and marrow. My life wasn't my own, and my body didn't belong to me . . . I lived solely for the Party and the Supreme Leader . . . I didn't experience joy, but I was filled with an unshakable determination to remain loyal, even to the point of death.[9]

> My life's goal was simple: to live in accordance with the Supreme Leader's will. But what was his will? It was to feed the North Korean people and create conditions for them to live well—messages that were constantly propagated through the media. I then asked myself, 'What do I need to do to fulfill his will?' This was how I thought and lived.[10]

Struggles to Comply with Forced Obedience

Two participants shared about the hardships they faced in their efforts to comply with the regime's forced obedience. One participant, LF, in her fervent adherence to the regime's ethical rules, reported her teacher to the Education Bureau for accepting expensive birthday gifts from some students. However, the outcome was devastating. Instead of punishing the teacher, the regime allowed LF to be ostracized by both the teacher and her fellow students. She recounted:

> The Supreme Leader was doing his best to feed the people, walking along the ridges between rice paddies at dawn without sleep. So, how could my teacher accept bribes and fabricate grades? I thought, 'How can the will of the Supreme Leader be fulfilled in this way?' The ethical rules for educators, students, and laborers were written in the Supreme Leader's instructions, just like in the Bible . . . My teacher was not living by those rules, so I reported her to the Education Bureau for accepting expensive birthday gifts from students. The result, however, was devastating.[11]

Participant IM remained loyal to the regime alongside his mother. When his father was sent to a prison camp for speaking about freedom, they were pressured to sever their relationship with him. IM recounted:

---

9. RF, Transcript, 1.
10. LF, Transcript, 1.
11. LF, Transcript.

They pressured me to accuse my father and cut ties with him. They said that if my mother divorced him, the consequences for me would be less severe. Despite this recommendation from the Party, I saw my mother remain steadfast, refusing to change [her mind]. I didn't know why [perhaps it was the LORD's protection]. I held my father in my heart sincerely.[12]

Enjoyment of the Privileges Granted to the Elite Class

In stark contrast to the harsh lives endured by most North Koreans, Participant DM shared that he belonged to the elite class in North Korea, enjoying exclusive privileges. From a young age, he deeply loved and admired the Supreme Leader. Over time, he ascended to a high-ranking position in the government, gaining both power and additional privileges. He recounted:

From my childhood, I set my life goal on reforming Chosun [North Korea] with strong conviction. I admired Kim Il Sung; whenever I attended his meetings, I couldn't help but confess that he was truly the greatest leader! As a commissar in the Party, I held significant power and enjoyed a life of influence.[13]

Uncertainty within the Rigid Social Hierarchy

Seven participants made 13 references to experiencing uncertainty within North Korea's rigid hierarchical system. They talked about systematic oppression, existential questions beyond Juche ideology, individualistic pursuits for personal gain, and experience of life in concentration Camps—sub-subthemes identified in the study.

Systematic Oppression

Four participants recounted feeling confused and uncertain about life, primarily due to their low status within North Korea's rigid social stratification system. Participant EF shared her experiences of discrimination and mistreatment because of her family's so-called "undesirable" or "miserable" background:

12. IM, Transcript, 3–4.
13. DM, Transcript, 1.

Findings

> My parents were outsiders because they had originally come from Japan. My father was taken away when I was 2 years old. We barely survived. They said, 'We are just taking care of you due to the Party's thoughtfulness, but you are different human beings than us.' They openly mistreated us.[14]

Participant HM described how his parents' Christian teachings at home conflicted with the regime's ideology, leaving him deeply confused:

> My father and mother even said that the North Korean regime would surely fall and that it was terribly going wrong... My grandfather told me not to join the Party because it adhered to idol worship. I was educated with Christian values at home, and my parents lived an exemplary life. However, publicly, I was taught materialistic philosophy. As a result, I became confused about my identity.[15]

Existential Questions Beyond Juche Ideology

Three participants shared that they experienced confusion and uncertainty in life due to unanswered questions that the ideology of Juche failed to address. The following reference illustrates their dilemma:

> Men are born into this world and die when their time comes... I always wrestled with questions in my mind: 'Do men live to eat?' 'Do we eat to live?' 'Why were we born into this world?' 'What is the purpose of my life?' These questions constantly haunted me. I was always curious but found no answers about the reason for living.[16]

Individualistic Pursuits for Personal Gains

Participant IM described how he shifted his focus in life to pursuing and accumulating personal gain after losing faith in the Party:

> I realized that there was no longer any hope in the Party and that I had been deceived all along. After deciding to live for myself, I discovered there was nothing I could actually do for myself... I started thinking about making money because this was before the

---

14. EF, Transcript, 1.
15. HM, Transcript, 1.
16. PF, Transcript, 1.

market changed. The only thing I thought could bring me happiness and that I could do for myself was to get married.[17]

In summary, nearly half of the participants acknowledged that the regime required their absolute loyalty to the Supreme Leader. More than one-third expressed disillusionment with the system. Their confusion and uncertainty, rooted in the rigid social hierarchical system of North Korea, ultimately played a role in their conversion, as many found answers in the Bible.

Life Experiences in Concentration Camps

Participant JF described her life in a prison camp as one of abandonment and isolation:

> When I was young, I lived in a prison camp where there was no one but us. We used to play in the yard, but the environment was miserable. I thought that only my grandmother, my family, and I existed in the whole world [because we had no contact with the outside world]. It was an isolated place devoid of love.[18]

Life's Goals and Values Under the Regime

Ten participants made 26 references to life's goals and values under the regime. These are further divided into two subthemes: Aspirations for Money, Freedom, Knowledge, etc., and Upholding Personal Values.

Aspirations for Money, Freedom, Knowledge, and More

Nine participants made 18 references to their life goals, which were categorized as aspirations for money, freedom, knowledge, nobleness, success, and the reformation of North Korea. Participant IM explained how thirsty he was to gain true knowledge, for he was without his father to instruct him. He read as many books as he could:

> Children normally don't read full-length novels, but it was possible for me due to my great thirst . . . I was moved by [the story

---

17. IM, Transcript, 13.
18. JF, Transcript, 1.

of] Kim Il Sung, and I was born again as a man of Kimilsungism
... It was truly a religion! The kingdom was [in me], but it was of
an idol.[19]

In contrast to those pursuing personal aspirations, Participant HM sought a path to reform North Korea:

> My father and mother explained many things about life using the stories from the Bible. All the time, I had questions about how I could change [North Korea]. Later, I found out that the answer was in the Bible ... Then I was able to understand why they [the regime] were persecuting and prohibiting people from reading the Bible.[20]

Upholding Personal Values (Conscience, Sincerity, etc.)

Five participants made eight references to their efforts to uphold core values such as sincerity, dignity, and living according to their conscience while navigating life in North Korea. Participant KF recounted her sense of pride and dignity, which stemmed from being recognized as fully devoted to the Party. Motivated by this pride, she refused to succumb to death by starvation in front of her family. Ultimately, this resolve led her to make the decision to defect from the country:

> I struggled because of my pride ... I couldn't bear the thought of dying of starvation in my family's presence because I was known for my loyalty to Kim Il Sung. My pride hurt so deeply ... I decided to defect instead ... Even if I were to die along the way, I thought at least I could preserve my dignity.[21]

This shared commitment to upholding core values—exemplified in his case by loyalty to the Party—was echoed by other participants, including IM:

> 'Who was I?' I existed solely to serve the Supreme Leader, the Party, and the nation. There was no place for 'I' within the system. I was the head of a working group. We worked tirelessly and raised a pig, using our own money ... We killed and ate it, but it turned out to be a violation of the Party's principles ... A Party secretary

19. IM, Transcript, 1.
20. HM, Transcript, 6.
21. KF, Transcript, 2.

reported it to the higher organization . . . One day, I sent him [the envoy] away after beating him.[22]

Those who spoke about their goals for knowledge, nobleness, and success ultimately devoted themselves to serving the Party, as it was the best and often the only means available in North Korea to pursue their aspirations. Unsurprisingly, after converting to Christianity, these individuals became deeply faithful and committed Christian leaders in South Korea.

Resulting Challenges

Fifteen participants made 77 references categorized under the theme of Resulting Challenges. This theme is divided into three subthemes: Trauma and Crisis-Induced Challenges, Mental and Emotional Challenges, and Interpersonal Struggles.

Trauma and Crisis-Induced Challenges

Fifteen participants shared 57 references regarding trauma and crisis-induced challenges: persistent feelings of hopelessness, powerlessness, erosion of human dignity, struggles with meaninglessness and low self-worth, uprootedness and dependence on relatives, struggles with identity crisis, extreme loneliness, and severe malnutrition from betrayal and persecution.

Three participants specifically expressed feelings of hopelessness rooted in challenging family backgrounds. One account illustrates this vividly:

> My father was considered a reactionary, and my family was labeled as part of an impure adversary class. I had no dreams. If I had had a dream, it would have been to shake Kim Il Sung's hand once, thinking that the event could possibly change my life. Actually, there were some people who took pictures with Kim Il Sung, and their lives changed . . . If possible . . . I thought about intentionally setting my house on fire and bringing out the portrait of Kim Il Sung, even at the risk of burning myself in the process. It could give me a chance to be on TV, and that event could bring changes in my life.[23]

---

22. IM, Transcript, 9–10.
23. EF, Transcript, 1.

Participant AF shared feelings of powerlessness, describing the absence of any institution or person to appeal to after having been captured by human traffickers:

> My life was miserable ... There was no one to turn to when injustice was done to me ... They sold and bought people illegally ... There was no place or person I could plead my case to.[24]

Another participant, a woman referred to as PF, described perceiving her life as entirely worthless and feeling that she deserved to die. She recounted how she struggled with a profound lack of self-worth and a sense of meaninglessness in her life:

> After the North Korean economy failed, I didn't know why I had to go on living. I had no hope in life ... I thought I should die. There was no meaning in my life.[25]

Participant TM recounted the devastation he experienced after his best friend betrayed him in prison. The betrayal left him deeply wounded:

> I made a friend in prison with someone my age. We almost became sworn brothers. We thought we would live and die together. We shared whatever we found on the ground, whether it was a piece of bean or a cabbage leaf. However, he betrayed me for a handful of rice. One day, he reported to the prison supervisor that I had picked up a cigarette butt from the ground and smoked it. In return, he received a handful of rice. After that, he persecuted me so badly that my weight dropped to 45 kilograms, and I was diagnosed with the third degree of malnutrition.[26]

Mental and Emotional Struggles

Ten participants made 24 references to their mental and emotional troubles. These challenges included emotional indicators of depression, heightened insecurity, and anxiety, and struggles with low confidence. One participant shared how depression led to violent behaviors:

---

24. AF, Transcript, 1.
25. BF, Transcript, 1.
26. TM, Transcript, 2.

> Every day, depression weighed on me so heavily that I beat my son. He was my idol, but when he disobeyed, I beat him. I acted violently toward others, both in actions and words.[27]

A male participant, IM, described his discouragement led to depression:

> I was the child of a political prisoner, disdained by others. I couldn't lift my face . . . I used to be proud of my father, but then he became a prisoner. Before I could even form my worldview, I experienced persecution . . . I went crazy when things didn't go as I expected . . . I lived like a bully and was eventually expelled from school.[28]

Another participant shared how crippling depression, manifesting as intense anxiety, profoundly impacted her life:

> I had a dream of freedom but no one to talk to. Despair always lingered in my heart. In other parts of the world, many people have religions to turn to in times of need, fear, or anxiety. But there, we couldn't have religion, and all superstitious activities were forbidden . . . I felt fear and anxiety about my future and yearned for freedom. I often asked myself, 'Why are we unhappy? Why am I unhappy?'[29]

For Participant CF, the symptoms manifested as low self-confidence:

> I was not a bright person. Perhaps it was because I had lived a hard life since childhood. I had no confidence. Whenever I compared myself to others, I felt incapable of doing anything . . . I struggled with my studies. I was physically weak and very thin. Even tasks that others could do easily were very difficult for me. I felt timid.[30]

Interpersonal Struggles

Five participants made eight references to interpersonal struggles, which were attributed to factors such as outbursts of anger, harboring revengefulness, spousal conflict, suspicion and hypocrisy, and poor physical health

27. BF, Transcript, 7.
28. BF, Transcript.
29. MF, Transcript, 2.
30. CF, Transcript, 1.

affecting relationships. One participant shared how his anger outbursts led to challenges in his relationships:

> My father passed away when I was 12 years old. After his death, my dream of becoming a general with stars on my shoulders fell apart. Around that time, a South Korean soap opera called *The Son of a General* became very popular among us students. Influenced by the gang fights in the drama, I got involved in group fights against students from other schools. We fought, drank, and spent time together without any thought for our futures . . . Eventually, I nearly beat to death the person who had arrested my uncle and caused his death through severe torture.[31]

A female participant recounted the distress she endured due to her husband's excessive alcohol consumption:

> I was mentally distressed. My husband drank, and his drinking habits were bad . . . Patriarchalism was prevalent in North Korea at the time . . . [The most difficult and fearful thing in my life was] our marital relationship. I ran away from home countless times.[32]

For MF, life in North Korea was sustained by hypocritical compliancy with the regime. As a result, when she met Christians in China, she struggled to trust their kindness and questioned the sincerity of their love:

> I [initially] suspected the genuineness of their love. Why? In North Korea, we showed fake love to one another. Everything we did was hypocritical. Even when we disagreed with the regime's teachings, we still had to study what they taught, carry out the work they commanded, and participate in their mandated activities . . . I had nothing I truly wanted to do . . . [After I defected to China] I didn't trust the Christians I met when they treated me like family, so I kept my distance. 'What's in their minds?' I wondered . . . In North Korea, I had been taught that religion takes everything from you as if cutting your heart out of your chest . . . I was so thoroughly indoctrinated that I kept rejecting their genuine love and constantly tested it.[33]

Thus far, the category of *Life Prior to Conversion* has been explored. Of the 20 participants, 15 made a total of 77 references to difficulties arising from trauma, crises, mental and emotional struggles, and interpersonal

---

31. TM, Transcript, 1.

32. FF, Transcript, 1.

33. MF, Transcript, 4.

struggles. The number of participants and their collective references illustrate the depth of their suffering. Notably, the majority of these references—57 in total—centered on crises experienced under the regime, during defection, and in transitional countries. This segment of the analysis reveals that the most frequently mentioned hardships were those related to trauma and crises. Participants' experiences overwhelmingly reflect the flaws, failures, and deceptions of the regime, as well as the dire conditions that followed. Additionally, all participants, to varying degrees, shared worldviews shaped by the North Korean context.

Despite their outward allegiance to the Supreme Leader, some participants began to question the regime while still in North Korea. DM, a high-ranking Party official who once enjoyed the privileges of the regime, became increasingly disillusioned by its injustice and indifference toward the people. His perspective shifted after secretly reading the Bible, ultimately leading to a profound transformation and faith in God. In contrast, HM, an elite participant raised with a Christian worldview, was never fully convinced by the regime's ideology. As he advanced within the government due to his intellectual achievements, he became more aware of its falsehoods and contradictions. Even while living under the regime, he resisted its control and longed for a more just society.

Other participants also encountered God while still in North Korea. EF experienced numerous miracles during her time there, and TM began spreading the gospel within the country after encountering God in China. JF, who was imprisoned in a concentration camp, had already started communicating with God before being baptized by a repatriated Christian. IM first heard the gospel through a radio broadcast and had a personal experience of God while still in North Korea. In total, 30 percent of the participants were significantly influenced by a Christian worldview before leaving North Korea. This underscores the profound impact of faith, even within the oppressive confines of the regime.

Motives of Conversion

This section aims to address the participants' motives for conversion, as these reasons could significantly influence their subsequent worldview transformation or change. The information was gathered and analyzed based on responses to the second question in the questionnaire: "What were your motives for converting to Christianity?" Axial coding identified

Findings

72 references, which were categorized into four main themes: Experiencing God, The Role of the Christian Community, The Role of Hardship, and Transcending North Korea's Restrictive Living Conditions through God's Grace. Each theme was further divided into subthemes for detailed analysis.

Table 8. Themes and Subthemes of Motives of Conversion
(P: number of participants; C: number of comments)

Category	Themes and Subthemes	P	C
Motives of Conversion	*Experiencing God*	20	46
	Experiencing God's Grace	20	41
	Personal encounter with God	16	27
	Community of Believers	6	16
	The Holy Spirit's Intervention	11	22
	Understanding God's Will and His Kingdom	7	13
	The Role of the Christian Community	16	45
	Fulfillment of Felt Needs	9	17
	Spiritual Enrichment through Sermons, Bible Studies &Media	9	10
	Guidance from Believing Family Members	5	9
	Influence of Verbal, Written, and Lifestyle Testimonies	4	13
	Faith Development through Training Programs	2	2
	The Role of Hardship	15	23
	Vulnerability from Lack of Safety, Security, and Provision	11	17
	Disillusionment with Trusted Ideologies	4	4
	Processing Painful Memories and Recognizing Sinfulness	1	1
	Transcending North Korean's Restrictive Living Conditions through God's Grace	10	24
	Appealing to a Supernatural Being	8	14
	Recognizing the Regime's Flaws and Failures	6	11
	Awareness of the World's Diversity	1	3

Experiencing God

Twenty participants made 46 references to the theme of Experiencing God. This theme highlights the relational essence of Christianity, which is designed to be lived out through relationships. While experiencing God often occurs within the context of community, it can also be a deeply personal experience, though not necessarily private. To provide clarity, the analysis considered all conversion cases in detail. The subthemes identified under this category are Experiencing God's Grace, The Holy Spirit's Intervention, and Understanding God's Will and His Kingdom.

Experiencing God's Grace

Among them, 20 participants testified 41 times to experience God's grace through personal encounters with him and within the community of believers—sub-subthemes identified in the study. One participant described witnessing God's power firsthand when his prayer for a miracle was answered:

> I told my pastor that I wanted to do a 40-day fast because I hoped for two things: that hair would grow on the scarred, empty spot on my head and that I would come to believe in God. However, at my pastor's insistence, I fasted for only 20 days. From the third day of fasting, my prayers began to change, and my heart grew desperate . . . I prayed, 'God, I want to believe in You, but I can't. Please give me faith.' On the 10th day, after the early morning prayer meeting and my quiet time, I went to the bathroom. As I was washing my face and looking in the mirror, I saw hair beginning to grow on the scarred spot. Overcome with joy, I ran to my pastor and exclaimed, 'Pastor, my hair is growing!' I leaned my head toward him, and he responded, 'Hallelujah. Isn't God alive?' The scar on my head didn't have pores, making it impossible for hair to grow there. [Out of shame, I had always covered the spot with hair from other parts of my head.] But now, with confidence, I started praying even more fervently, and my hair grew rapidly. Typically, hair grows about 1 cm per month, but between the 10th and the 20th day of my fast, the empty spot was completely covered with hair.[34]

PERSONAL ENCOUNTER WITH GOD

Sixteen participants made 27 references to experiencing divine grace through the Holy Spirit's Intervention, Answered prayers, and The scriptures. One participant shared how God personally revealed himself to her in a dream as the One who was pierced on the Cross for her sins and who knew her name, ultimately leading her to Jesus:

---

34. TM, Transcript, 8.

> He told me about Jesus for two hours. I didn't believe him, saying, 'How can a dead person come back to life?' I thought such a thing could never happen. However, that very night, I had a dream of Jesus coming to show me his pierced palms and feet. As he was being lifted up to heaven, he called my name and asked, 'Can you now believe me?' Since then, my eyes were fixed only on Jesus, and my life began to change.[35]

Participant GF described experiencing God's healing power through the Holy Spirit during a church service:

> As the church service ended and I stood up, lifting my arms from the bench, I felt as though my legs and body were floating . . . I started crying. Since I was imprisoned in China and repatriated to North Korea, I have always felt something heavy embedded in my chest. Suddenly, I felt it was gone. I felt so light, like a feather floating in the air . . . Later, I realized that this was a Holy Spirit experience.[36]

Six participants described 11 accounts of experiencing God's grace through answered prayers. They include the provision of daily necessities, safety during defection, miraculous healing, and reunion with a lost child. In addition, they also spoke of experiencing grace through God leading them to conviction of sin as experiencing God's love and realizing that God was present in their past suffering. In particular, Participant, AF shared that she had cried out to God in prayer, asking why she had endured such deep shame and pain. She opened her heart to Jesus after realizing that God had been with her even in her most traumatic and painful moments:

> I escaped to China when I was 17 years old. I asked God defiantly, 'Why did I have to be sold around [by human traffickers]?' Even in North Korea, I had been sexually abused since my youth. Feeling mortified, I asked God, 'Why [did all these things happen to me]? Didn't you say you loved me? . . . If so, why?' . . . I heard God's voice saying, 'When you were weeping and in pain, I was always there with you . . . I loved you so much that I bore the cross, taking on your shame and the terror you endured.' At that moment, I collapsed. I had always been abandoned and mistreated, but now I realized there was at least One Person who truly loved me and had been with me all along! I wept uncontrollably . . . From that point

---

35. GF, Transcript, 3.
36. RF, Transcript, 3–4.

on, I began to search for him. For the first time in my life, my heart opened to him, and my life began to transform.[37]

Participant EF's testimony involves God answering her prayers by providing for her during her dire circumstances in North Korea:

> The woman I met in China gave me one hundred Yuan and asked me to write down the LORD's Prayer and the Apostle's Creed on paper. She told me to pray them repeatedly when I returned to North Korea, saying that God answers our prayers... After I used up the money she gave me, I ran out of rice. Remembering my promise to her, I prayed to God with all the doors closed and covered with blankets... I read the LORD's Prayer slowly, one word at a time, and the end, I prayed, 'God, I am hungry. Please take care of my rice. I pray in the name of Jesus. Amen.' That was my first prayer, and I went to sleep that night. The next morning, I opened the door and found 2 kilograms of noodles outside. It felt like an earthquake in my head. Who could have brought them to me?... The next time, I prayed the same prayer, and the following day, a woman who sold rice in the market called me. She handed me a sack of soiled rice, explaining that her bag had broken the previous night as she was bringing it into storage after returning from the market. She didn't have time to clean it and told me to take it and eat it... I thought, 'There must be something to this!' From then on, I prayed to this God, and he answered me in so many different ways. Food was provided to me for one and a half years. Later, when I read Romans 10, I realized that the reason God answered my prayers was probably because I confessed with my mouth, even though I didn't yet have faith. He responded to my prayers according to my confession. Even now, when I look back, I am amazed by all the prayers he answered.[38]

Six participants mentioned six accounts of experiencing God's grace flowing through reading the Bible. Participant HM, an elite in North Korea, testified about experiencing God through the Word while in China. This experience brought him to a deeper understanding of the Christian knowledge his father had shared with him back in North Korea. He described how God granted him supernatural intellectual insight, enabling him to understand the Bible in just 14 days. This profound comprehension allowed him to discern the falsity of the heretical teachings his boss was

---

37. AF, Transcript, 5–6.
38. EF, Transcript, 3–5.

trying to lure him into with promises of various benefits. Above all, HM found answers in the Bible about how to bring change to North Korea. This discovery led him to place his faith in God and dedicate his life to the cause:

> For 14 days, I immersed myself in reading the Bible . . . My understanding underwent a supernatural transformation. I recalled Hegel's theism and the biblical stories my father had told me during my childhood. These pieces of knowledge became logical and systemized in my mind. For the first time, I understood why North Korea strictly bans reading the Bible . . . I longed to return to North Korea with the Bible in hand. During this time, my boss introduced me to the leadership of a heretical group. They claimed that Jesus would return to Earth at 4 p.m. on April 4, 2004—something that clearly contradicted what I had read in the Bible. I debated with them and won . . . Even so, their top leader offered me an opportunity to study in Canada, but I turned it down because I knew their beliefs were not aligned with biblical truth. After coming to faith in God, my vision for changing North Korea became clear. I was no longer afraid but filled with confidence.[39]

Likewise, Participant OM experienced God's grace while reading the Bible and came to comprehend and accept that Jesus shed his blood on the cross for the forgiveness of his sins:

> God made us his children, and the most moving part for me was realizing that he sent his Son, Jesus Christ. Since then, I continued drawing closer to God. However, the decisive moment in my conversion came when I understood that it was the blood of Jesus Christ that opened the way to God—something that was not possible during the time of the Tabernacle in the Old Testament . . . This revelation caused the Bible to open up to me in an entirely new way. At that moment, I was overwhelmed and nearly cried. I said, 'I finally understand!' From then on, my personal relationship with God grew deeper and deeper.[40]

Community of Believers

Six participants referred to experiencing God's grace within the community of believers 16 times, particularly through having their needs met and

---

39. HM, Transcript, 2.
40. OM, Transcript, 4–5.

observing the words and lifestyles of missionaries. Participant NM shared that the greatest factor in his transformation came from witnessing the exemplary lives of missionaries marked by kindness in the transit nation:

> The group of people I first met in the church were missionaries. How different they were! It was the missionaries who brought about the greatest change in me . . . I had never encountered such people in my life . . . Their words were so tender and gentle. They ate the same food we ate . . . potato soup and kimchi . . . We shared meals, sang hymns, and they prayed for us . . . These missionaries came from South Korea and Canada—Korean diasporas. Whenever we sang hymns and prayed together, they kept saying, 'My nation, my nation!' I wondered why they prayed for North Korea. Why were they crying and praying with tears for my country? It puzzled me, yet it felt so refreshing . . . How on earth could such a situation exist?[41]

The Holy Spirit's Intervention

Eleven interviewees referenced their experiences of God through the Holy Spirit's intervention 22 times. Many of these accounts have already been described under the subthemes of Experiencing God's Grace and Understanding God's Will and His Kingdom. Experiences such as miraculous healing, conviction of sin, encountering the love of God, and receiving callings played a significant role in their conversion. Here is one additional example:

> They protected me and provided housing at no cost . . . When I needed clothes, they brought them for me. Wow! Is this paradise? I felt like I was floating on clouds . . . One day, they told me it was time to be baptized. I dressed nicely for the occasion . . . During the service, we had communion and baptism, and we read the Words, 'By his wounds, we are healed.' Wow! My heart burned so fiercely inside me that I could hardly contain it. I kept asking myself, 'Why in the world did this person, Jesus, die for me?' I couldn't fully comprehend it, but I was so thankful that I cried . . . God sent his Son for a sinner like me, and these people protected me so that I could come to know his name . . . It was so moving! I felt that this was the day of my conversion.[42]

---

41. NM, Transcript, 5.
42. TM, Transcript, 8.

FINDINGS

As such, all participants encountered God through various experiences, such as through the work of the Holy Spirit, answered prayers, Bible reading, and witnessing the Words and lifestyles of missionaries within the community of believers. Ultimately, the essence of these experiences was God revealing his loving and forgiving nature, as well as his will for their lives. This profound revelation enabled the participants to welcome God into their hearts as their LORD and Savior.

Understanding God's Will and His Kingdom

Seven participants described their understanding of God's will and his kingdom 13 times. Participant TM shared that he received God's call after experiencing miraculous healing in the transit nation:

> God revealed to me a scene of Moses leading the Israelites across the Red Sea. He whispered in my ear, referencing Exod 3:10, 'So now, go. I am sending you to Pharaoh to bring my people, the Israelites, out of Egypt.' At that moment, the Holy Spirit struck me, and I fell to the floor, overwhelmed with conviction. For two days, I repented, rolling on the floor, and began speaking in tongues . . . Then, I received a call from the LORD. I said, 'I need to preach the gospel to North Korea and lead the people to God.' I carried a sack full of Bibles and various teaching materials into North Korea. This is how I encountered God.[43]

Participant OM shared that his worldview was completely transformed when he discovered the kingdom of God through reading the Bible, which he realized held the power to bring positive change to North Korea:

> I thought I could be safe if I could get a student Identification [card] from the school that they were mentioning. I went there struggling. It was a Bible reading class of a pastor, Choi. I thought that I was deceived and tried to go back home the next day. However, I gave a chance and remained there to read the Bible. I found about God's world in it and I could say that my worldview was totally changed then . . . I found answers to the desperate questions I had. 'Why does North Korean people live like this?' 'How can I save North Korea?' The love of Jesus Christ! The principle of nonresistance teaches us to turn the other cheek if anyone slaps us on the right cheek! I found a biblical paradigm of God's kingdom operating quite differently [from other systems]. I realized that

43. TM, Transcript, 8.

God could change North Korea... North Korean people strived to survive by hating and trampling on one another. If North Korean people accept God's rule and system, North Korea will become a wonderful society.[44]

The Role of the Christian Community

Sixteen participants shared experiences that align with the theme of the Christian community, totaling 45 references. This category is divided into five subthemes: Fulfillment of Felt Needs, Spiritual Enrichment through Sermons, Bible Studies, and Media, Guidance from Believing Family Members, Influence of Verbal, Written, and Lifestyle Testimonies, and Faith Development through Training Programs.

Fulfillment of Felt Needs

Nine participants made 17 references to coming to the Christian faith after experiencing God's provision in times of need. The needs they mentioned included well-being, finances, and healing, the gift of faith in God, opportunities for education, refuge and safety, and freedom from the guilt of sin. One participant described how she encountered God while seeking refuge and safety, stating:

> I wasn't sure if it was Shenyang or another place, but I heard people saying that an identification card could be issued if you participated in a Bible study.[45]

Another participant said that she believed in Jesus all the more when her need for freedom from guilt was met:

> The more I came to know Jesus, the more I realized the depth of my sin. This understanding led me to place my faith in him even more.[46]

---

44. OM, Transcript, 2.
45. PF, Transcript, 3.
46. CF, Transcript, 2.

Findings

Spiritual Enrichment through Sermons, Bible Studies, and Media

Nine participants made 10 references to coming to the Christian faith by discovering the sacrificial love of God, the biblical paradigm of God's kingdom, answers to questions about life, and by repenting of their self-centeredness. One participant, who found answers to her questions about life through a sermon, described her experience:

> I went to a small village church led by a single female pastor. As she began preaching from the book of Proverbs, I felt as though I was being pulled into a black hole, like in a movie. It was because her words answered the questions that had weighed heavily on me: 'What do people live for?' 'Did we come into this world just to live like this?' 'Why do we live worse than pigs and dogs?' It felt strange to find these answers in a church. Even though I didn't yet have faith in God, I decided I would attend the church.[47]

Another participant experienced Jesus' sacrificial love through a movie he watched in China.

> I watched the *Jesus* movie in a Chinese village. At the end of the film, when Jesus was crucified with large nails driven into his hands and feet, I felt as though those nails were piercing my own heart . . . Until that moment, I had lived only for myself and my family. But who in the world would live and die for others like Jesus? Tough people like me and my friends lived by loyalty to one another. If one of us stole a loaf of bread, we would share it among the group . . . A relationship bound by duty and trust. All three of us were moved to tears at the final scene of Jesus' death on the cross. He died for us—so now, what should we do? It became clear: a duty-bound relationship with Jesus.[48]

Guidance from Believing Family Members

Five participants made nine references to their motives for embracing the Christian faith, citing influences such as a family member's guide to faith, being reminded of a trusted grandfather's faith, and intercession. These are sub-subthemes identified in the study. One participant shared how her grandfather's influence led her to trust the believers she met in China.

---

47. SF, Transcript, 3.
48. NM, Transcript, 4.

> I was deeply surprised when they began singing *Amazing Grace* because my grandfather used to sing that song to me every morning, placing his hands on me as I left for school [back in North Korea]. I asked, 'Why am I hearing the same song here?' My memory of the song was vivid because my grandfather had raised me. One by one, I started recalling his unusual habits, like taking me to the mountain with his backpack every Sunday. It finally dawned on me that my grandfather had been a Christian all along. I respected him more than anyone else, and I thought, 'If this was the God he believed in, then I have nothing to lose by believing in the same God.'[49]

Influence of Verbal, Written, and Lifestyle Testimonies

Four participants made 13 references to coming to the Christian faith by observing the selfless and sacrificial lives of missionaries, finding peace of mind even in the midst of trouble, discovering vision, hope, and dreams in God, and witnessing the exemplary lives marked by kindness. One participant shared how she experienced Jesus through reading books of testimonies:

> The elder of the group home gave me a bag full of books containing testimonies from the 1960s Christian revival that transformed the South Korean church. I read *Pastor Yang Won Son, Ki Chul Joo, history of Korean Women Christians*, and *Hallelujah Ah-Joom-Ma* ... For an entire week, I read these books without sleeping, weeping the whole time. 'What incredible stories!' I thought to myself. 'How can such moving stories even be possible? They were stories about God. I realized that the God of these people is my God. With this God, I can live—I can have dreams and hope. I can give my whole life to him.' For the next six months, I couldn't stop crying.[50]

Participant TM described how deeply he was impacted by witnessing the love of Christ demonstrated through a missionary's actions:

> [I caught the thieves and beat them until they bled . . . thinking they needed to be punished.] What the missionary did next completely shocked me. He untied the thieves and knelt before them, asking for their forgiveness. The thieves looked confused, unable to understand what was happening. The missionary told

---

49. AF, Transcript, 4.
50. MF, Transcript, 5.

them he was sorry, admitting that he hadn't taken the time to ask what they truly needed but had instead given them whatever he thought they should have. He said he was the one who caused the trouble and humbly asked for their forgiveness. Then, the thieves admitted they were in the wrong and knelt before him as well. Everyone began apologizing to one another, and the thieves broke into tears. The missionary and I couldn't hold back our tears either. I was stunned. 'How can a person be this good?' I could never have imagined such a scene. In North Korea, I believed it was right to beat people and take whatever you could from them in times of desperation. It was also normal to think that thieves deserved to be beaten. Watching this unfold, I couldn't help but wonder about the God the missionary believed in. I thought, 'I want to try believing in him too.'[51]

Therefore, this analysis indicates that nearly all participants came to the Christian faith through interactions with Christian communities in transit nations. The most frequently referenced factors were Fulfillment of Felt Needs and Spiritual Enrichment through Sermons, Bible Studies, and Media by the Christian communities. It is noteworthy that God used the community of believers in transit nations as his instruments for the salvation of North Korean defectors. Through these communities, God's nature was demonstrated by meeting the participants' needs and delivering his message of salvation through various means. This enabled the participants to encounter God personally, discovering a new sense of hope and peace in him.

The Role of Hardship

Fifteen participants reported 23 instances of hardships that influenced their conversion. These hardships included Vulnerability from Lack of Safety, Security, and provision, Disillusionment with Trusted Ideologies, and Processing Painful Memories and Recognizing Sinfulness. Although only 15 participants explicitly mentioned hardship as a contributing factor to their conversion, for North Korean defectors, hardship is generally regarded as a shared context or a common reality. First, they risked their lives to defect. Second, upon arriving in China, they faced an inherently illegal status, leaving them without safety, security, or provisions. They lived under constant threat of arrest and repatriation. This research, however,

---

51. TM, Transcript, 5.

focuses on the participants' subjective experiences of hardship—both mental and physical—that directly contributed to their conversion.

Vulnerability from Lack of Safety, Security, and Provision

Eleven participants made 17 references to their vulnerability from lack of safety, security, and provision, which were factors that contributed to their conversion. Their hardships included desperation for a refuge, anxiety over a loved one's repatriation, and desperation to find missing children, among others.

Participant MF shared her desperation to find refuge, which led her to pray and ultimately encounter the LORD:

> We had nowhere to go . . . No one welcomed us. We were not citizens of the [transit] country, living outside the safe boundaries, always ready to run at any moment . . . The desperation of our situation and the love shown by these people, who insisted that we must believe in God to live truly, created deep conflict within us . . . Our goal was simple and clear: survival . . . They claimed that God could give us life . . . But how? Their concept of life was rooted in the freedom found in the eternal truth of God. My understanding of survival, however, was entirely different. To me, survival meant having basic freedoms within a safety line—the kind of freedom that people in secure places like South Korea have . . . They told us to pray to God.[52]

Participant FF clearly stated that the reason she turned to God was her need for refuge:

> I had no one to turn to. God was my refuge. At that time, I had nowhere to go, no place to find comfort. That was why I believed in God.[53]

Participant RF described her desperate prayer to an unknown God for a safe defection to China. Later, she realized it was the Christian God who answered her prayers:

> I defected to China once and was repatriated to North Korea. After I had come out of prison, I wished to go back to China! When there was no one around, I kept looking up to the sky, pleading

---

52. MF, Transcript, 4.
53. FF, Transcript, 3.

for help . . . When people were not around me, I even made a low bow, pleading for help to cross the river safely and not be captured. I didn't even know that it was to God [I was praying to]. I did it out of desperation rather than adhering to a religion then . . . In the National Intelligence Service, there came a day dedicated to religion . . . They mentioned God . . . I was wondering if the North Korean sky I was pleading to was the God they mentioned . . . I said that I would attend the service where God was.[54]

Disillusionment with the Trusted Ideologies

Four participants made six comments about the hardship caused by the disillusionment with trusted ideologies, which ultimately contributed to their conversion. They expressed disappointment at the Party and a realization of having lived as a slave under the regime. Participant QF explained that her family was very loyal to the regime. However, when she was informed that her grandmother had starved to death, she became deeply disillusioned with the Party, leading her and her husband to search for alternative ways of living:

I was notified that my grandmother had passed away . . . I visited her tomb and made a decision . . . North Korea starves to death the loyal subjects . . . I said, 'If I go on trusting this regime, my children might die too.' This was the moment I changed my attitude toward the regime . . . My husband said that the regime exploited us. They didn't pay us but just threw a bag of candies and salt cookies on Kim's birthday as if they had done all their duties for us. What they gave us for one month's salary was less than one kilogram of rice . . . I was really disillusioned with them.[55]

Processing Painful Memories and Recognizing Sinfulness

Participant NM was a *kotjebi*[56] while living in North Korea. As such, he was forced to live alone in dire poverty. Surprisingly, this condition was

54. QF, Transcript, 1–2.
55. RF, Transcript, 2.
56. Behnke, *Kim Jong Il's North Korea*, 95–97. They are abandoned by their parents for various reasons, leaving them as orphans. The term *kotjebi* refers to homeless children in North Korea and translates to "fluttering swallows," a metaphor that reflects their constant search for food and shelter.

not what he considered a real hardship. After defecting to China, he lived with missionaries and other defectors, studying the Bible in a small shack while constantly facing the threat of arrest. He recalls that time as the happiest period of his life because he was surrounded by his (spiritual) family. However, the true hardship he faced was not physical but mental. For he struggled with the painful memory of his deceased siblings and the burden of acknowledging his past sinfulness as a habitual pickpocket. He kept this part of his life hidden from others and resisted admitting to himself that he was a sinner:

> The more I learned about God, the more I remembered those who died, shedding tears of blood. The more I came to know about God, the more I felt pain and sorrow because my shame was exposed . . . Even though I tried to erase my memories, the more I read the Bible, the more they came alive . . . I didn't like the phrase, 'You are a sinner,' in the beginning . . . I was rebellious . . . However, [ironically] the greatest factor that changed me was that same phrase . . . [Later,] I could 100 percent identify with it . . . Without even realizing it, I was saying to myself, 'Ah, yes, I am a sinner.' I was changing slowly.[57]

Altogether, more than half of the participants encountered God through the hardships they experienced. Their vulnerability due to a lack of safety, security, and provision opened their hearts to receive help and the gospel from faith-based communities in the transit nation(s). Additionally, the mental anguish caused by the disillusionment with trusted ideologies, along with the pain and acknowledgment of past sins, also played significant roles in their conversion.

Transcending the North Korea's Restrictive Living Conditions through God's Grace

Ten participants made 24 references to the theme of Transcending North Korea's Restrictive Living Conditions through God's Grace. This theme is divided into three subthemes: Appealing to a Supernatural Being, Recognizing the Regime's Flaws and Failures, and Awareness of the World's Diversity.

---

57. NM, Transcript, 4.

FINDINGS

Appealing to a Supernatural Being

Eight participants shared that they looked to a supernatural being or God for various reasons, including curiosity about God, a vague belief in a supernatural being capable of doing what humans cannot, seeking refuge, finding Christianity aligned with a desire for nobility, and desperation for blessings. One participant expressed curiosity about the Christian God, described as the Judge of the most vulnerable, such as orphans and widows:

> Even in North Korea, a god is mentioned . . . In moments of urgency, we pray to a god or to heaven for help, even without understanding the implications of such an appeal. So, I had a vague sense of a divine being's existence, but believing in a god—or in God—was clearly seen as an act of defiance. They said that Christians are those who disrupt and overturn the nation. The lady I met in China said that North Koreans were punished because they didn't believe in God. However, if they believed in God, they could live well. She also said that God is the Defender of orphans and widows. At that moment, I thought, 'Aren't orphans and widows the most miserable people in the world? What kind of God cares about such people?' Kim Il Sung didn't care about them. The loyal Party members only stood by the side of the distinguished. I wondered, 'What kind of God is he to be the Defender of the miserable?'[58]

Another participant described that her desperation for receiving blessings led her to search for God:

> I wasn't sure if this God was the same as the sky my mother used to pray to when she wished for a son . . . My life was so difficult that I saw myself as an unfortunate, unlucky, and miserable woman. That was why I ended up being repatriated to North Korea . . . The constant hardship and misfortune left me feeling like my heart had shriveled inside. I neither smiled nor laughed. In fact, I couldn't even bring myself to smile or laugh . . Still, I thought that maybe God would bless me if I turned to him.[59]

---

58. EF, Transcript, 3.
59. RF, Transcript, 2.

Recognizing the Regime's Flaws and Failures

Six participants made 11 references to the regime's flaws and failures, which led them to look beyond their circumstances and search for alternative ways of life and deliverance for the North Korean people. Four participants expressed disappointment with the leader and communism, which drove them to seek guidance from fortune-tellers or explore other paths in life. Two participants sought ways to rescue the people from misery in North Korea and to bring about the regime's downfall.

One participant shared that, in her desperation and disappointment with the regime, she felt powerless to save the dying youth in North Korea. At that moment, she was reminded of a Bible verse she had read long ago in China and heard God's voice telling her that he was the One who could bring help to the situation:

> There was nothing I could do as an adult when I saw little children dying on the streets. It was miserable. During *Arduous March*, many children begged me for food, but all my energy was focused on surviving myself, and I had no choice but to turn them away. It was a world where adults could not function as adults . . . I wanted to become an adult who could help [the miserable children] . . . In 2004, I reached a breaking point when I saw young soldiers, aged 17 to 27, on the brink of death from starvation and severe cold. The LORD reminded me of John 14:6, a Bible verse I had read in 2000 when I visited China to meet my uncle. I remember feeling like Jesus was speaking directly to me: 'Aren't you in pain over this situation? If you tell me what you feel and want, I will speak to God on your behalf.' I wept and wept. I was able to understand the Word because I was searching for a way.[60]

Participant RF explained her disappointment at the Party, which made her profoundly anxious about her future and led her to plead to the God whom she did not know:

> I trusted the Party and worked hard, but I became deeply disappointed in it . . . Eventually, I defected . . . When I felt lost because of my disappointment with the Party, I became very anxious about my future, even though they claimed I was the master of my own life. The Arduous March was incredibly difficult, and I constantly worried that I might die. I couldn't see any future ahead of me,

---

60. JF, Transcript, 1.

and my anxiety grew. I went to a fortune-teller, but they were not always accurate. So, I looked up to the sky and pleaded for help.[61]

Awareness of the World's Diversity

One participant expressed how his curiosity about other parts of the world led him to encounter Christianity, stating:

> This was our chant: 'We need to escape from this falling airplane, called Chosun [North Korea], as soon as possible!' We needed to look beyond . . . I secretly took with me a novel called *Gone with the Wind*, which was the first foreign novel I ever read. Since then, I have read many novels from Russia, China, and other parts of the world without knowing where those countries were . . . After I got married, we moved to a place called Hae Ryung. I was still looking outside vaguely and wanted to quench my thirst for the world beyond my physical boundaries by listening to the radio. The clearest frequency was coming from Far East Broadcasting Co., Korea . . . [As I was listening to it] God came to me—whose life was like a piece of pebble that even pigs trample. He came to me, the one no one even cared about . . . I started seeing a new world . . . Every dawn, whenever I heard the hymns from the radio, peace came upon my heart. At least in that one moment, who cares about ideologies?[62]

Recapitulation of this section indicates that half of the participants expressed a desire to look beyond the system imposed on them. As the ideologies they once trusted and the North Korean regime failed them, their despair led them to seek and appeal to a supernatural being—God. Ultimately, God guided them to experience his saving grace. This longing for something beyond ordinary means of deliverance often aligned with opportunities to encounter faith in a communal setting, where both their physical and spiritual needs were met.

80 percent of the participants indicated that their motives for conversion were rooted in experiencing genuine community, particularly when their needs were met and when they listened to sermons, teachings, or watched movies in a communal setting. Additionally, searching for a god who could do what they could not and dissatisfaction with the North Korean regime contributed to their conversion motives.

61. RF, Transcript, 2.
62. IM, Transcript, 14–15.

One noticeable feature was that several participants' conversion was not a shift from atheism or Kimilsungism to Christian faith but rather an internal transformation. As mentioned earlier, the Participant HM was influenced by his Christian parents' worldview, and God had been part of his perspective since birth. However, the Bible stories he had heard during childhood came alive only when God revealed himself to him as his personal Savior and LORD during a dire situation in China. Similarly, Participant JF, who was born in a North Korean prison camp, learned to connect with God even before fully realizing that the One she was speaking to and hearing from was God. Later, while recalling a Bible verse she had read during her time in China—that God can help the dying young people she desperately wanted to aid—she decided to be baptized by a repatriated North Korean believer while still in the North. These cases illustrate transformations that occurred internally rather than as dramatic shifts from one belief system to another.

The most frequently mentioned themes centered on experiencing God's grace and understanding his will. As shown in Table 8, 100 percent of participants reported encounters with God at the time of their conversion. These encounters brought about transformations in their worldview, particularly regarding cognitive themes such as the nature of God as love (40 percent), the Savior (35 percent), the One who reveals himself and communicates with his chosen (30 percent), and the One who convicts sin and enables repentance (20 percent).

In terms of self-identity, 35 percent of participants gained an understanding of God's will or call for their lives at the moment of conversion. This underscores that encountering God, who reveals his loving nature and engages with his chosen, enabled them to be cleansed and to open their hearts to receive him as their Savior and LORD. Moreover, for those who felt lost and without direction in life, discovering God's will or call played a transformative role in their journey to faith.

Immediate Changes Following Conversion

This section examines the participants' relatively immediate changes following their conversion, contrasting these with the longer-term transformations they experienced as their worldview evolved. The data were collected and analyzed from responses to the third question in the questionnaire: "In what ways did your life change after your conversion?" Axial coding revealed 65 references, which were organized into three main themes: Transformation in Understanding of God and Self-Perception, Transformation in Lifestyle and Life Goals, and Transformation in Attitude toward Others. Table 9 below outlines these themes and their subthemes.

Table 9. Themes and Subthemes of Immediate Changes Following the Conversion
(P: number of participants; C: number of comments)

Category	Themes and Subthemes	P	C
Immediate Changes Following the Conversion	*Transformation in Understanding God and Self-Perception*	18	36
	Experiencing New Emotions	16	27
	Developing a Biblical Understanding of God	10	15
	Gaining a Renewed Understanding of Self	6	7
	Transformation in Lifestyle and Goals	14	35
	Adopting a New Lifestyle	9	22
	Practicing spiritual disciplines	5	9
	Establishing the right priorities	4	9
	Reinterpreting past suffering	3	5
	Pursuing Life Goals Aligned with God's Kingdom	9	14
	Focusing entirely on North Korea	6	10
	Preaching the gospel	2	2
	Living for God's glory	1	2
	Transformation in Attitude toward Others	6	10
	Cultivating a Generous Heart	4	6
	Building Stronger Relationships	3	3

Transformation in Understanding God and Self-Perception

The theme of Transformation in Understanding God and Self-Perception has three subthemes: Experiencing New Emotions, Developing a Biblical Understanding of God, and Gaining a Renewed Understanding of Self.

Experiencing New Emotions

Sixteen participants shared 27 references to experiencing new emotions following their conversion. Of these, nine participants made 14 references to feelings such as peace, security, freedom from fear, and comfort.

Additionally, participants described emotions like joy, hope, a sense of brightness, and increased confidence. Some notable examples of these experiences include the following:

> God answered all my prayers. Then, I thought that he was my real Father who answered my prayers. 'Is there anything I should be afraid of?' Previously, I thought that money was the best thing I could have... My God is rich, and I can become rich too [laugh] ... My heart became generous... My depression was gone.[63]

> He [Jesus] came back to life in 3 days. I said, 'I knew it!' 'How can God die?' He shouldn't die. He can't die. This faith suddenly became mine, and I felt so secure that I thought I only needed to believe in him! God is eternal, and he never dies even if I die.[64]

> As I had a conversion experience, I realized that I was a sinner in need of God. I realized that he chose me to preach the gospel to North Korea for him. I was just happy. As I shed tears of joy, I realized for the first time how beautiful the sky was and how beautiful the leaves were. Why? Because I had only rushed madly forward in the past.[65]

> Once I encountered God, I found hope [in him]: 'What if I die now? What if something happens to me, like getting sick or having an accident?' Regardless, I didn't think that I would be sorrowful.[66]

Developing a Biblical Understanding of God

Ten participants shared 15 accounts of how their understanding of God was transformed through developing a biblical perspective of God. They, therefore, spoke of him as the Provider God, the Father God, the God of love on the cross, the Master and Creator, the living and eternal God, and the God who is working in North Korea. Note Participant QF's testimony as an illustration of this development:

> My husband asked me if we could go and help the broadcasting company for North Korea without pay. I said that he was crazy. I

63. BF, Transcript, 6–7.
64. RF, Transcript, 4.
65. KF, Transcript, 3.
66. CF, Transcript, 2.

might have said 'yes' if my husband had been earning some money for our family. At that time, I was struggling to provide for the family on my own . . . However, after I met the LORD . . . [eventually] we went there to work . . . God started providing . . . Someone gave us transportation money, and another person helped with our holidays. At the beginning of this job, we said that all we needed were rice, bean paste, and soy sauce, but there was nothing more we could ask for because everything was provided [by God].[67]

So many people are living on the face of this earth, and 'Why me, LORD?' I asked. Why do you give me such grace and let me know your love? This love I could neither understand nor handle. When this love was poured into me, I got to love others as well, naturally.[68]

I was striving to make an underground church in North Korea . . . The moment I realized that God was already working in North Korea, I said, 'Isn't it You who are living? You were the one who called and encountered me.' Since then, my confession has changed.[69]

Gaining a Renewed Understanding of Self

Six participants made seven references to gaining a renewed understanding of themselves. They described a newfound understanding of their new identity in God, God's calling, and their sense of being precious and worthy. Below are two examples illustrating the participants' renewed self-perceptions:

> I listened to some of his sermons, and he talked about how precious I am to God and who I am in his eyes . . . I used to think of myself as miserable and insignificant. However, after I met the LORD, I realized how precious and blessed I truly am [laugh]. I used to feel sad because I had nothing. Even though I still don't have material things like money or parents, the greatest One is with me, and I don't worry much about anything else. Now, my mind is renewed.[70]

---

67. QF, Transcript, 5.
68. SF, Transcript, 4.
69. IM, Transcript, 16.
70. AF, Transcript, 6, 11.

> I realized that my life no longer belongs to me—it is his. Whether I live or die is entirely in God's hands. As long as I live, I am to live for his kingdom. It was a total transformation. Previously, I believed I deserved to die and that I must die, but now I have come to life. I am here to live for God's kingdom and his gospel. Now, I have hope.[71]

Transformation in Lifestyle and Goals

The theme of Transformation in Lifestyle and Goals is divided into two subthemes: Adopting a New Lifestyle and Pursuing Life Goals Aligned with God's Kingdom.

Adopting a New Lifestyle

Nine participants shared 22 accounts of adopting new lifestyles. Among them, five participants described nine instances of practicing spiritual disciplines, including pursuing the knowledge of God, prayer, and obedience to God's lordship. Four participants described shifts in their priorities, while three shared how they gained new understanding from the LORD about their past suffering, including imprisonment for their work for God's kingdom. Below are some examples of the references they made about their new lifestyle after conversion:

> I was very thirsty [to know God]. After I finished reading the Bible from Genesis to Revelation once, the deacon was very happy to lend me 14 spiritual books . . . I cried so much as I was reading them . . . I continued my journey to Vietnam with the Bible in my possession . . . Before coming to Korea, I read the Bible 50 times.[72] Previously, money was the most important thing in my life. Now, I focus on finding ways to please God.[73]

> I came to understand only after being released from prison why God allowed me to be imprisoned. [God said,] 'It is not you, but I am the One who does the work.' Through the missionaries to whom I distributed the Bible, many families heard the gospel, came to faith, and the number of believers grew. The reason God

---

71. PF, Transcript, 7.
72. KF, Transcript, 3–4.
73. CF, Transcript, 2.

allowed my imprisonment was to teach me to trust him and witness the work he does.⁷⁴

Pursuing Life Goals Aligned with God's Kingdom

Nine participants reported 14 instances of their transformed life goals, now centered on fulfilling the kingdom of God. Of these, six participants made 10 references, specifically highlighting their unwavering focus on the mission to reach North Korea. The remaining participants stated that their primary goal was to live for God's glory and preach the gospel. Below are two examples of the new life goals they embraced after their conversion:

> I prayed, 'God, I now understand the way that humanity must go. You are the beginning and the end, and I now understand Your way . . . It is neither the way of communism nor the way of capitalism. It is only Your Way that is absolute! I will live for it. Your Word, the Bible, should be translated into North Korean so that they can know Your Way. Let me do the work.'⁷⁵

> After I met God in Korea . . . I realized that I was to live for God's glory, whether I eat or drink, as the Bible says . . . In my preparation to enter college, I always prayed and thought about ways to give glory to God through my major, Youth Guidance . . . [Also,] I enjoyed praise and worship a lot. I wanted to serve God by playing a musical instrument . . . I took drum lessons and played the drums for his glory.⁷⁶

Transformation in Attitude toward Others

Six participants shared 10 accounts that fall under the theme of Transformation in Attitude toward Others. This theme is further divided into two subthemes: Cultivating a Generous Heart and Building Stronger Relationships.

---

74. TM, Transcript, 10.
75. DM, Transcript, 4.
76. AF, Transcript, 8.

Cultivating a Generous Heart

Four participants shared six accounts of their transformed attitudes, particularly their growing capacity to practice generosity toward others. They described cultivating a more compassionate and accepting heart. Two participants provided the following examples of this transformation:

> I felt compassionate toward those who do not know God, even if they have more money and better positions than I do. 'Since they do not know God, . . . aren't they going to hell if they continue on their own way?' Previously, I felt bad for those who didn't have food to eat or clothes to wear, but now I feel bad for those who do not know God.[77]

> I became relaxed. We used to be very guarded against others and self-conscious, but now I have changed to embrace and accept them.[78]

Building Stronger Relationships

Three participants mentioned three times their changed attitude toward others, highlighting their ability to build stronger relationships. Below is how these two participants described the change:

> I was about to treat my son violently, but I stopped, remembering God's Word. Previously, I used to regret it after beating my son, but now my character has changed a lot.[79]

> When I looked into the Ten Commandments, I slapped my lap. It says to honor your parents. The North Korean Ten Principles, with all their details, are all about Kim Il Sung. However, the Ten Commandments speak about honoring parents and loving neighbors, which overwhelmed me and caused unceasing tears to flow.[80]

The key discovery of this section is that the participants experienced significant changes in self-perception and their understanding of God following their conversion experiences. Their lifestyles and life goals shifted noticeably, as did their attitudes toward others. These transformations were

---

77. CF, Transcript, 4.
78. OM, Transcript, 3.
79. BF, Transcript, 7.
80. KF, Transcript, 3.

particularly evident in their emotional lives and their conception of God. As a result, their lifestyles and life goals were clearly redirected toward a God-centered focus and a pursuit of the kingdom of God.

Life after Conversion

This section examines the information collected from participants about their lives after conversion, with a particular focus on the challenges they faced during their process of worldview transformation. The data was derived from responses to the fourth question in the questionnaire, which asked, "What areas of your life have you found challenging to transform since your conversion?" Through the axial coding, 145 comments were identified and grouped into four themes: Limited Understanding of God, Self, and God's Kingdom, Mental, Emotional, and Relational Difficulties, Residual Effects of the North Korean System, and The Burden of Life in South Korea. Table 10 delineates the themes and subthemes related to the lives of participating North Korean defectors after their conversion.

Table 10. Themes and Subthemes of Life after Conversion
(P: number of participants; C: number of comments)

Category	Themes and Subthemes	P	C
Life after Conversion	*Limited Understanding of God, Self, and God's Kingdom*	19	50
	Struggles in Submitting to God's Lordship	18	41
	Harboring criticism and/or unforgiveness	9	22
	Idolizing missions in NK, children, self, and money	8	12
	Dependence on social welfare and capitalist market	2	5
	Prioritizing personal needs	2	4
	Clinging to the old self	1	1
	Persistence of Unbiblical Views of God	5	9
	Feeling Alienation/Marginalization in South Korean Churches	2	2
	Mental, Emotional, and Relational Difficulties	18	47
	Anger, Bitterness, and Hatred	11	20
	Relational Difficulties	12	20
	Depression, Loneliness, Fear, and Pain	6	8
	Ungodly Pride	2	2
	Residual Effects of the North Korean System	11	31
	Emphasis on Self-Reliance and Humanism Rooted in Juche	8	21
	Blind Obedience Stemming from North Korean Idolization	2	3
	Utopian Ideals Rooted in Nationalism	2	3
	The Burdens of Life in South Korea	7	11
	Financial Struggles (Including Remittance to North Korea)	6	7
	Stress from Education and Lack of Formal Schooling	1	4

Limited Understanding of God, Self, and God's Kingdom

Nineteen participants shared comments about the challenges they faced due to a limited understanding of God, self, and God's kingdom during the process of worldview transformation. The subthemes identified include Struggles in Submitting to God's Lordship, Persistence of Unbiblical Views of God, and Feeling Alienation and Marginalization in South Korean Churches.

Findings

Struggles in Submitting to God's Lordship

Eighteen participants provided comments that are classified under the theme of Struggles in Submitting to God's Lordship. In particular, they mentioned harboring criticism and/or unforgiveness, idolizing missions in North Korea, children, self, and money, dependence on social welfare and capitalist market, prioritizing personal needs, and clinging to the old self—sub-subthemes identified in the study.

Harboring Criticism and/or Unforgiveness

Nine participants acknowledged struggling with harboring criticism and/or unforgiveness toward others. One participant shared her experience of frequently criticizing fellow defectors, stating:

> About the North Korean defectors, I wondered why they lived like that. If they worked hard, they could live well, like my husband, who earns good money through hard work. 'Why don't they work instead of begging from others?' I hated them and gossiped about them. Their lives were so disorderly and immoral—they fornicated and lived together without marrying, and they didn't seem to care. I was so angry that I hated and criticized them, thinking it was acceptable in the name of 'justice.'[81]

Participant IM highlighted unforgiveness as a significant challenge he faced during his journey of worldview transformation:

> When he said the word 'forgiveness,' it reminded me of many people back in North Korea. 'If you were me, would you be able to forgive those who took away your father?' I mean 'those who starved to death 3 million people, including my family.' I kept asking God, 'How can I forgive that person who continues to tear apart my family even now?' 'Have you ever experienced seeing your child being thrown into a pit?' When they asked us to declare 'forgiveness of the cross' over our lives, my self-righteousness arose, and I said, 'If this is the kind of God you are talking about, I am done with him, and I don't need to meet him!'[82]

---

81. EF, Transcript, 11.
82. IM, Transcript, 15.

From Juche to Jesus

Idolizing Missions in North Korea, Children, Self, and Money

Eight participants found that North Korea-related ministries, children, themselves, and money became idols in their lives. Participant IM expressed repentance for turning North Korea ministries into an idol:

> North Korea was my idol, and its ministry as well ... I confessed this in front of many people ... I used to preach because of North Korea, I prayed because of North Korea, and I didn't do anything unless it was related to North Korea. The sorrow and sadness of North Korean defectors had become obstacles ... Instead of being bound to Jesus, we were unknowingly bound by our pain and sorrow.[83]

Another participant also struggled with the same challenge:

> There were still unsolved issues even after some time had passed ... Feeling pain for my people and about my past [in North Korea] ... Most of the power in our lives comes from that pain. For example, when we say we will do ministry for North Korea, many times it is not out of sincere love for God but rather from the painful feelings [we have] toward the suffering people there ... When my time in prison was almost up, I realized that I was more of a patriot than a Christian and more of a nationalist than a disciple of Jesus.[84]

Participant RF's struggle centered on her inability to break free from self-imposed oppression. In North Korea, Kim had been the master of her life, but after her defection, she became her own master. Still, she struggled with self-imposed oppression and frequent emotional outbursts directed at herself and her family. She was trapped by her own emotions and a relentless need to control what was beyond her power:

> Once I make a plan and it doesn't produce the result I expect, I cry. I still have this tendency, though it has faded now. [The root cause is that] I made myself an idol ... Another example is how I wished my son would follow my instructions... It was difficult for me ... I vented my anger. My anger and beating didn't work ... I turned around and regretted it.[85]

---

83. IM, Transcript, 18.
84. OM, Transcript, 3–5.
85. RF, Transcript, 8.

Findings

Dependence on Social Welfare and Capitalist Market

One participant emphasized how her reliance on social welfare and the capitalist market as a foundation for a good life became a challenge in her worldview transformation, as it drew her away from dependence on God:

> Previously, I experienced many deficiencies in my life. A difficult task assigned to me at work caused me to struggle greatly . . . [After coming to Korea], I delivered newspapers, sold Yakult, and worked in restaurants . . . Over time, I began longing for easier, more comfortable work . . . This growing desire for comfort gradually led me to distance myself from Jesus.[86]

Another participant, TM, described a similar difficulty:

> While attending university and learning specialized welding at Polytech, I acquired assets in the process . . . Money started coming into my pocket. I bought a car, had a baby, and set up an installment savings plan. As I began saving money, I quit going to the early morning prayer meetings and became a Sunday Christian.[87]

Prioritizing Personal Needs

According to Participant JF, she struggled between prioritizing her personal needs over God's kingdom matters. She described her struggle between attending Discipleship Training School (DTS) at *Youth With a Mission* (YWAM) and addressing the urgent financial needs of her family members in North Korea:

> The person asked me if I really wanted to meet God. He suggested that I go to the University of the Nations on Jeju Island . . . On the first day at the school, they confiscated my phone, but I was anxious, worrying that my children in North Korea might try to contact me . . . At 10 o'clock at night, I stood in the middle of the flags in the courtyard, surrounded by darkness. I couldn't see my future at all. I looked up at the sky filled with stars and started to cry . . . 'Why am I here, LORD? My children and husband are waiting for me to send money to them . . . Why am I here, LORD,

---

86. FF, Transcript, 7.
87. TM, Transcript, 11.

leaving behind all these people?' Korea [Korean government] has given me only 500,000 Won over the past six months.[88]

Clinging to the Old Self

Participant QF identified clinging to her old self as a hindrance from being transformed into a mature Christian:

> I realized that the young people quickly accepted the truth taught from the Bible by the deaconess. I didn't understand why I wasn't grasping anything . . . After the teacher and my children went to bed, I went to the living room and opened the material she used to teach us. One illustration she shared was about a glass full of water. No matter how much water you pour into it, nothing will go in because the glass is already full. At that moment, something dawned on me. Young people are pure, but I was full of myself. Even though I had defected and abandoned the country, I was still holding tightly to my own things, whether they were good or bad, being completely full of myself.[89]

Persistence of Unbiblical Views of God

Five participants reflected on the challenges they faced in their worldview transformation, particularly their struggles with breaking free from unbiblical views of God. They described perceptions such as an angry and coercive God, a God who does not keep his promises, a God confined to North Korea, and a God indifferent to dying children. One participant, who once believed that God was indifferent to the suffering of children in North Korea, recounted the following story:

> The most challenging question I couldn't resolve was about the suffering and death of children [in North Korea]. Adults die because of their sins, but what sins have children committed? If you were in my position, you would ask the same question . . . My sister died, my classmates died, and even those who used to sell goods with me at the train station died . . . Our society was collapsing because adults, proud of their immorality, abandoned their children—the very

---

88. JF, Transcript, 3.
89. QF, Transcript, 2–3.

products of that immorality. 'What is God going to do about this kind of sin?' I relentlessly questioned God, demanding answers.[90]

The same participant shared his thoughts about a God who does not keep his promise of protection. The sincere leaders of the mission shelters in China, where he stayed, were arrested by the Chinese police. The participant himself was also arrested three times. He described the harrowing experience in these words:

> It was the year 2003. I was interrogated for a year by the North Korean Security Agency after being labeled an absconder to South Korea and classified as a political criminal. During this time, I began to lose my faith in God. Didn't they say He is a God who protects? 'What does He mean by protection?' I was captured three times because of him—the One who promised to protect me. Before I became a Christian, I was never captured . . . 'What kind of God is he?' I asked. I had no one to turn to. My father had passed away, and I had nothing left. Yet, despite it all, I found myself still praying to God, clinging to a faint hope.[91]

Feeling Alienation and Marginalization in South Korean Churches

Two participants remarked on specific characteristics of South Korean churches that caused them to feel alienated and marginalized, creating obstacles to their worldview transformation. One of them mentioned the following:

> One day, I saw them praying and wailing for the finance needed to construct a new church building. I couldn't understand all this because I just came from seeing the dying children in North Korea . . . As soon as I finished the [six months] discipleship program, I said, 'Amen,' and ran away from the church . . . Our God is left behind in North Korea. I prayed to God that I would make lots of money [here] and glorify his name after I go back to North Korea . . . When speaking to a friend, I mentioned that I believe God's presence is limited to North Korea and that my intention is to earn money here in South Korea.[92]

---

90. NM, Transcript, 6.
91. NM, Transcript, 5.
92. JF, Transcript, 2.

As outlined above, most participants encountered significant challenges in their worldview transformation due to their limited understanding of God, themselves, and God's kingdom. In particular, their struggle to submit to God's lordship became a major obstacle in this process. For North Korean defectors, submitting to God's authority was especially difficult. In North Korea, their master had been the Kim family. After defecting, they became their own masters. However, upon coming to Christ, they once again faced the challenge of shifting their allegiance—this time to Jesus.

However, without fully surrendering to God's lordship, they found it impossible to experience true freedom or peace. Throughout this journey of constant transformation, many personal idols they harbored were exposed, leading them to further purification and transformation. Additionally, distorted views of God had a profound impact on some participants. One participant, NM, whom I mentioned above, was so affected by an unbiblical perception of God that he abandoned his faith for 8 years.

Mental, Emotional, and Relational Difficulties

Conversion is both an instantaneous event and an ongoing, lifelong process. Even after conversion, Christians continue to wrestle with moral and psychological struggles that affect both themselves and their relationships with others. This section explores the mental, emotional, and relational difficulties described by 18 participants. Specifically, they reported struggles with Anger, Bitterness, and Hatred. Others spoke of Relational Difficulties, as well as experiences of Depression, Loneliness, Fear, Pain, and Ungodly Pride.

Anger, Bitterness, and Hatred

Eleven participants reported struggles with anger, bitterness, and an inability to forgive, which they attributed to factors such as hatred, contempt, indifference, and injustice, and resentment. They also identified the absence of a father and economic collapse, lack of love, and low social status as the reasons behind the strong negative emotions they harbored. Participant EF, for instance, expressed that she was filled with anger due to the hardships she faced as a result of her family's low status in North Korea's social stratification system:

> How happy I was! Where in the world was a place like South Korea? All things were possible by just pushing buttons. I didn't have to go fetch water. All day long, I could use warm water. The toilet is inside the house. I just had to push a button to cook rice. It was paradise! An overwhelming joy kept me crying. When I went to church, I cried. I couldn't believe that I was [finally] in South Korea! This overwhelming feeling didn't last 6 months . . . As I was stabilized and had enough food to eat, anger started rising within me. Wow! It brought me so much trouble. When I saw my husband, I got irritated. When I saw my kids, I got angry.[93]

Participant JF reported feeling angry when South Korean ministers dismissed or undervalued her successful ministry solely because she was a North Korean defector:

> The North Korean defector ministry [I led] was experiencing a revival. However, it was looked down upon and dismissed as insignificant [by South Korean ministers]. I felt angry when I was alone. Sometimes, I would call my friend and start cursing them out of frustration . . . I don't get angry at North Koreans but only at South Koreans:[94]

Another participant mentioned her tendency to tenaciously pursue those who falsely accuse her because of resentment:

> Whether it was when I had faith in God or not, I couldn't handle it whenever people falsely accused me. Even though I didn't do a certain thing when someone accused me of doing it, . . . I used to pursue that person even if it meant to the end of the earth . . . However, since I came to the Christian faith, the level of my fierceness has come down.[95]

Participant PF explained feeling bitterness toward her stepmother because she was abusive back when they lived in North Korea:

> I was raised by my stepmother. I was really oppressed by her and never was allowed to talk back [to her] . . . As soon as my father left home for work, she cursed and beat me. [Her abusive treatment] laid a bitter root within me . . . My teachers liked me and sent me to a training class close to my graduation. I liked going there

---

93. EF, Transcript, 7.
94. JF Transcript, 5.
95. LF Transcript, 7.

because I didn't want to go home to face my stepmother . . . All I wanted was to leave home.[96]

One male participant described holding unforgiveness issues as follows:

> I was still burning with revengeful thoughts toward my friend who betrayed me. However, I did not recognize it until [the LORD touched me] while I was in the Plumb Line session [a healing program in YWAM's DTS].[97]

Relational Difficulties

Classified in this category of relational difficulties are the stories of twelve participants who shared their struggles in relationships with others. Seven participants made 10 comments specifically about their challenges with South Korean Christians, while ten participants made 13 comments about relational difficulties in general. Here below is a female participant who described her conflict with the associate pastor of the South Korean church she attended:

> This friend of mine was so envious and jealous of me that she turned people against me . . . She had her daughter lead the worship [without my permission, even though I was in charge of church administration]. I realized she had teamed up with the associate pastor . . . I was consumed by anger and turned everything upside down . . . I said, 'I won't go to this church anymore!' . . . When the associate pastor called me, I cursed at him, saying, 'You xx! You don't even understand God's order . . . I don't believe you! Don't call me again!' I didn't want to deal with someone who had no understanding of God's order . . . He was my authority figure . . . I felt uneasy about what I had done.[98]

Participant GF referenced experiencing discrimination by South Korean Christians as follows:

> It seemed like they were excluding me . . . I didn't want to harbor any ill feelings toward them, but I couldn't help but feel saddened, questioning whether they would treat me the same if I weren't from North Korea. There was a moment during an international

---

96. PF, Transcript, 11.
97. TM, Transcript, 11.
98. PF, Transcript, 10.

conference when Korean individuals were given the opportunity to speak. My team leader distributed the microphone and the right to speak among the team members, leaving me out . . . It made me feel disheartened.[99]

For Participant SF, the strained relationship she endured involved her spouse:

> My husband threatened to kill me with a knife and pull out my teeth with cutting pliers. I shouted back, 'Kill me!' Other people saw me as a pastor, but I questioned myself, 'Am I a woman of faith?' My heart was so far from God's, but I chose to cast my anxiety on him and trust . . . I realized there was such wickedness in my heart.[100]

Participant KF also shared the strained relationship she had with her husband:

> It was the third time he had put me in a stranglehold . . . I had already experienced this before and sat down to ask my husband, 'Did you try to kill me?' He said, 'Yes!' His eyes were bloodshot, and he didn't look well. However, strangely, I remained calm. It was my final breakthrough in this spiritual battle. I comforted my husband, saying, 'You must have been going through a difficult time [these days].' It was true that he had no one to rely on . . . My husband replied, 'That's why I asked for a divorce from you.' The second reason he wanted a divorce was because I was crazy about Jesus. But I responded by asking him, 'Am I a true Christian?' At that moment, his eyes started trembling, and I saw his mind waver . . . Then, I said, 'Thank you' and 'Thank you for thinking of me like that.' Suddenly, the atmosphere completely changed.[101]

Depression, Loneliness, Fear, and Pain

Six participants made comments regarding their difficulties caused by depression, loneliness, and fear. One participant spoke about her struggles with depression and loneliness, particularly when reminded of her mother and siblings still in North Korea, and recognized that she had no one to confide in:

> I acted irritated toward my husband and my son . . . Depression came upon me . . . I had no relatives here . . . I had my second

---

99. GF, Transcript, 9.
100. SF, Transcript, 12.
101. NM, Transcript, 7.

> baby and missed my parents in North Korea . . . My husband came home only on weekends because he was a driver . . . To me, my new house [in South Korea] was heaven at first, but now it felt like a cave or even hell . . . My life was settling here, but I kept being reminded of my past miserable life, my miserable parents and siblings back in North Korea . . . 'Who am I now?' I was becoming 'the old miserable self' again . . . My son asked me why I kept walking around instead of going home . . . I had nowhere to go . . . I had no one to talk to . . .[102]

Participant CF suffered loneliness after arriving in South Korea. Her story is:

> The most difficult part of a defector's life in South Korea is loneliness. Few of us defect as a family unit, and many come here alone. It is hard to stand alone, especially emotionally . . . When I see people around me in relationships, I hear Satan whisper in my ear, 'Are you lonely? Here is a good man.' This became a real struggle for me.[103]

For Participant CF, who had experienced abandonment throughout her life, the fear of being abandoned again remained. She was even afraid that her pastor would leave her:

> When I met the pastor after coming back from China, the first thing I said to him was, 'Pastor, do not abandon me, please!' I was abandoned [by people] all my life . . . This word to the pastor suddenly came out of my mouth in my desperation.[104]

Ungodly Pride

Two participants made comments about their struggle with ungodly pride. Of them, a male participant, HM, revealed how prideful he has been since his childhood, stating:

> Until now, I feel automatically prideful whenever I successfully do the things that ordinary people can't.[105]

In summary, the data analysis for this section indicates that most participants faced challenges related to mental, moral, and relational difficulties during

---

102. EF, Transcript, 7–8.
103. CF, Transcript, 6.
104. AF, Transcript, 4.
105. HM, Transcript, 4–5.

their worldview transformation. Notably, 11 participants acknowledged struggles with anger, bitterness, and unforgiveness, while 12 participants reported having relational difficulties. Specifically, 7 out of 12 participants (58 percent) experienced both anger-related and relational difficulties, suggesting a connection between these struggles. Additionally, among the 7 participants who faced challenges in their relationships with South Korean Christians, 5 (71 percent) also reported other relational difficulties.

Eighteen participants identified mental, emotional, and relational difficulties during their worldview transformation process. Of these, 15 participants had experienced mental, emotional, traumatic, and relational difficulties before conversion. Thirteen participants shared common themes. This means that 87 percent (13 out of 15) of those who had previously suffered from trauma and emotional distress continued to struggle with these issues throughout their worldview transformation. On average, these 13 participants had been Christians for 14 years, indicating that mental, emotional, and relational difficulties have remained significant challenges in their journey of worldview transformation.

Residual Effects of the North Korean System

The process of worldview transformation was marked by significant struggles for many participants, particularly due to the lingering influence of the North Korean system. Eleven participants made 31 comments regarding the difficulties encountered in this process. The key subthemes identified were Emphasis on Self-Accomplishment and Humanism Rooted in Juche Ideology, Blind Obedience Stemming from North Korean Idolization, and Utopian Ideals Rooted in Nationalism in contrast to the kingdom of God Jesus preached.

Emphasis on Self-Accomplishment and Humanism Rooted in Juche Ideology (Criticism, Hostility, etc.)

During the process of worldview transformation, many participants struggled with deeply ingrained patterns of self-reliance and humanism shaped by Juche ideology. Eight participants made 21 comments about the difficulties they faced in moving away from these beliefs. Their testimonies highlight the challenge of shifting from a worldview centered on self-accomplishment to one of dependence on God. One participant, EF, reflected on how Juche ideology had influenced her understanding of faith, even after conversion:

> We used to believe in Kim Il Sung as a god, and many of the obstacles to believing in God stemmed from the worldview that he was always with us . . . He was like a god living in us. Even those who had once devoted their lives to him after coming to the Christian faith seemed to serve God in the same way. Like many other defectors, I was no different. [For example,] believing in Kim Il Sung meant doing my best, obeying his command, and proving my loyalty through my actions. However, believing in God is not about what 'I' do first but about obeying his Word and following his will . . . When we act, we are to pray first and be led by him, but most defectors believe they must act first, and God will eventually help them.[106]

> Two million people in North Korea are thoroughly imbued with anger, hatred, and hostility. The regime brainwashed us with slogans such as 'Let's smash down the invaders!' and 'Let's put an end to South Korean puppetry!' Every day, we were required to chant these slogans, and over time, they took hold of us . . . When we see other people, our first instinct is to find their weaknesses because of the habit of criticism ingrained in us through the *Saenghwalchonghwa* Life Review Sessions.[107] When I go to church, I instinctively notice people's faults first . . . Many defectors are still dominated by anger, hatred, and resentment . . . Unless this issue is addressed, everything becomes a target for their hostility. If someone who was once kind to me changes her attitude even slightly, instead of trying to understand, I immediately see her as an adversary. In North Korea, there are only two kinds of people: white or black. Those labeled as gray [fence-sitters] are considered spies.[108]

Another participant acknowledged her struggle with a deeply ingrained habit of criticism:

---

106. EF, Transcript, 12–14.

107. Ministry of Unification, "Life Review Sessions." A mandatory weekly meeting in which individuals review and reflect on their thoughts and actions according to the teachings of Kim Il-Sung, Kim Jong-Il, Kim Jong-Un, or the Ten Principles. Every North Korean citizen is required to participate in these Life Review Sessions within their affiliated organization or Party group. The process involves both self-criticism and mutual criticism.

108. EF, Transcript, 12–14.

Findings

> I believed in God's Word 100 percent, but my biggest struggle was my habit of criticizing and condemning others. In North Korea, we constantly criticized each other, and I was even the one leading the Life Review Sessions . . . Criticism would come out of my mouth automatically, like pressing a button on a vending machine.[109]

For some, the emphasis on self-accomplishment also extended into their Christian ministry, often at great personal cost. One male participant shared how his commitment to church work led to marital conflict:

> I was constantly at the church—eating, sleeping, and working there—without going home. My wife asked me, 'Aren't your children your sheep?' and 'Who am I [to you]?' But even amid conflict with my wife, I believed I was doing the right thing because the church members praised me and treated me well . . . I thought church ministry was the first priority in my life. Meanwhile, my wife and I kept arguing. When she asked me to step back from church ministry, I refused and asked, 'Aren't you a Christian?' and 'Isn't it your duty to take care of the children?' Finally, my wife said, 'Let's divorce.' I responded, 'Even if we divorce, I can never let go of my ministry in the church.'[110]

Participant OM, who had previously acknowledged that missions in North Korea had become an idol in his life, reflected on his efforts during his 10-year imprisonment in China. During this time, he reevaluated his striving in light of God's kingdom work in North Korea. He recognized that he had been relying on his own efforts instead of allowing God to work through him. He concluded that God alone should carry out his work in his own way, using him merely as a vessel so that all glory would belong to God:

> I was imprisoned in China for 10 years because I was involved in evangelism, rescuing defectors, and helping them reach South Korea . . . I struggled against God while in prison . . . That time in prison became a turning point in my faith. My greatest struggle was questioning whether my past faith had been right. I had loved God and believed that he should change the land [North Korea]. I was willing to give my life for it . . . But I asked myself, 'Was I right?' 'Did I live according to your will?' 'Did I do well?' In the Bible, Jesus' disciples focused on him, thinking he would save them from Roman rule. My focus was exactly the same. I still harbored hatred toward North Korea deep in my heart. I had to let it

---

109. KF, Transcript, 4.
110. TM, Transcript, 13.

go . . . Gradually, I realized that what I had thought was right was actually wrong. Then what? I had to deny the very righteousness I had lived for—even though it was the strength that had carried me through my years in prison. It felt as if my soul had left me . . . I realized that I desperately needed to seek the living and true God, which brought me unbearable anguish.[111]

Blind Obedience Stemming from North Korean Idolization

Two participants made three comments regarding their struggle with blind obedience, which they attributed to the deeply ingrained culture of idolization in North Korea. One participant described this challenge as follows:

> When I talk with my children, I realize that I think within a narrow frame of thought [shaped by my upbringing in North Korea] . . . When I ask my kids to do something, and they strongly express their opinions, it makes me really angry . . . Now, as I study education and social welfare, I have learned that it is not wrong for children to freely express their opinions to their parents about whether they can or cannot do what is asked of them . . . However, when it comes to my Christian faith, I find myself expecting the same kind of strict, North Korean-style obedience from my congregation.[112]

Utopian Ideals Rooted in Nationalism

Two participants made three comments about their struggle with utopian ideals rather than Jesus' teachings on the kingdom of God. They recognized these ideals as obstacles to their worldview transformation. One of them shared the following perspective:

> As soon as I came to Christian faith, the purpose of my life became to raise funds . . . The organization I work with is focused on changing North Korea by connecting and mobilizing churches there. The kingdom of God is going to come to North Korea sooner than to South Korea because South Korea is under the control of mammon . . . I want to establish a university [in North Korea] . . . with a new leadership composed of Korean elites and

111. OM, Transcript, 4–5.
112. MF, Transcript, 6.

God-centered, pure people . . . I will gather North Korean defectors along with the people inside North Korea.[113]

Although this participant expressed a strong desire to serve North Korea, the researcher observed that his understanding of the kingdom of God and the nature of God remained limited.

In total, 11 participants identified aspects of the North Korean system as obstacles in their process of worldview transformation. Among them, 8 participants (73 percent) specifically highlighted their struggle with self-accomplishment and humanism rooted in Juche ideology. The research also revealed that 5 out of these 8 participants (63 percent) had lived lives of total allegiance to the Supreme Leader before their conversion to Christianity. Additionally, 8 of the 11 participants (73 percent) who identified the residual impact of North Korean ideology as a challenge had also lived under total allegiance to the Supreme Leader before coming to faith. The findings suggest that those who had been more deeply committed to the regime before conversion experienced greater difficulties in their worldview transformation due to the lingering influence of the North Korean system.

Burdens of Life in South Korea

Seven participants commented on the burdens they faced while adjusting to life in South Korea, particularly in the areas of financial distress and academic challenges.

Financial Struggles

Six participants shared their personal struggles with financial hardship, primarily due to the responsibility of sending remittances to family members in North Korea. Additionally, the pursuit of theological education placed further strain on their finances. These challenges often became a source of temptation, diverting them from their pursuit of God's purpose in their lives. Nevertheless, they testified that the LORD graciously provided for them, opening avenues of support and provision.

One participant, JF, described the tension she experienced between her theological training and her urgent financial responsibility to her family in North Korea:

---

113. HM, Transcript, 7.

> Someone asked me if I truly wanted to meet God and suggested that I go to the University of the Nations on Jeju Island . . . On the first day at school, they confiscated my phone, but I felt anxious, wondering if my children in North Korea might try to contact me . . . At ten o'clock at night, I stood in the middle of the courtyard, surrounded by flags, in the darkness. I couldn't see my future at all. I looked up at the sky, filled with stars, and started to cry . . . 'Why am I here, LORD?' My children and husband are waiting for me to send money . . . 'Why am I here, LORD, leaving them behind?' The Korean government has only given me 500,000 won for the past six months.[114]

Another participant, JF, described how he obeyed God's calling to pursue theological studies despite severe financial hardship:

> I entered seminary . . . But reality was very different . . . I had no money . . . I complained to God, saying, 'What are you doing, God? You told me to enter the seminary.' Around that time, I met my wife . . . I told her that I had neither a house nor a car—I was practically a beggar. But she still thought of me as a good person. We lived in the dormitory of the school, which was the biggest blessing from the LORD. Without that housing, we would have faced enormous difficulties and dangers . . . But making a living was not easy . . . The money my wife had saved for 3 years before marrying me was used to pay off my debts. We lived in constant financial struggle. We attended Bible study, and I focused on my coursework. We also received some financial support from the government. But for 3 years, we had nothing.[115]

Stress from Education and Lack of Formal Schooling

As detailed thus far, many participants faced significant challenges in adjusting to life in South Korea, particularly in the areas of education and employment. For those who had little to no formal schooling in North Korea, the transition to an academic environment was especially difficult. Participant BF's experience illustrates the struggles faced by those attempting to rebuild their lives through education. Having been unschooled in North Korea, she faced significant challenges in adapting to an academic environment. While in a transit country, missionaries instructed her not

---

114. JF, Transcript, 3.
115. NM, Transcript, 7.

to lie during her interview with the National Intelligence Service, and she obeyed. However, as someone without a formal education, finding a job in South Korea was difficult. Even after she began studying, the overwhelming academic challenges left her feeling stressed and depressed to the point of experiencing suicidal thoughts:

> It was very difficult and stressful to study in Korea . . . I must have been depressed . . . 'What should I do?' I couldn't keep up with my studies . . . I thought about jumping from the window [of my house], but when I saw my son, I couldn't die and leave him behind. At that moment, I said to myself, 'I should pray!'[116]

The aforementioned participants' testimonies clearly reflected the burdens of life in South Korea. Although facing these challenges was never easy, all of them ultimately experienced God's help. The systems they had once belonged to were vastly different from the one they were now navigating—the kingdom of God. The stressful periods in their lives may have felt as if everything they once believed to be true was crumbling, but in reality, the LORD was working to build something new within them.

The examination of *Life After Conversion* revealed that 95 percent of the participants identified their limited understanding of God, self, and the kingdom as challenges in their worldview transformation. Additionally, 90 percent . . . (18/20) stated that their untransformed lordship over their lives was a key struggle. Their allegiance had transitioned—from the Kim family in North Korea to themselves, and finally, after conversion, to the LORD Jesus Christ.

Anger, bitterness, hatred, unforgiveness, and relational issues were also identified as significant obstacles. Furthermore, more than half of the participants recognized the residual impact of the North Korean system as a major hindrance in their worldview transformation. Participant MF, in particular, described the unique challenge of breaking free from the North Korean communist ethos, which demanded total submission to the regime's totalitarian system. Less than half of the participants (7/20) expressed experiencing the burden of life in South Korea. Despite these difficulties, some of them came to see that God was working through their struggles for their good.

In light of Hiebert's emphasis on total transformation at the worldview level, it is evident that, even after conversion, the participants continued

---

116. BF, Transcript, 10.

to struggle with various difficulties without fully experiencing a complete shift in worldview. They remained in need of God's transformative work to heal past wounds, remove inner hindrances, and lead them into a biblical understanding of God and his will so that they could fully embrace a biblical worldview.

Growth in Understanding of God, His Will, and Perspectives

This section presents data collected from responses to the fifth question, "How did you overcome these difficulties?" and the sixth question, "How did the transformation of your worldview into a Christian perspective occur?" The data was analyzed collectively to gain a comprehensive understanding of the participants' overall experiences of worldview transformation. While the most meaningful insights were derived from responses to the fifth question, not all of the data directly reflected a transformation toward a biblical worldview. Genuine transformation, however, begins with God's Word, as his kingdom is established and governed by it.

Findings

Table 11. Theme and Subthemes of Growth in Understanding of God, His Will, and Perspectives (P: number of participants; C: number of comments)

Category	Themes and Subthemes	P	C
Growth in Understanding of God, His Will, and Perspectives	*God's Intervention*	20	86
	Scripture (Reading, Meditating, Memorizing) and Praying	15	44
	The Work of the Holy Spirit (Voice, Wisdom, Vision, Healing, etc.)	13	39
	Other Means of Encountering God (Will, Hardship, Hymns, and Biological Father)	3	3
	Receiving Enlightenment and Knowledge of God	20	76
	Revelatory Insights	14	42
	Corrections	15	28
	Guidance	5	6
	Facing Challenges and Longing for Transformation	18	53
	Inner Struggles for Sanctification	11	21
	Seeking God's Kingdom and Perspective	9	14
	Desiring a Deeper Relationship with God	8	15
	Repentance for Spiritual Renewal	18	38
	Resistance to God's Lordship	10	18
	Immorality and Spiritual Negligence	5	8
	Self-Reliance & Self-Righteousness	4	7
	Anger, Bitterness, and Hatred	4	5

This section explores how participants experienced God's presence through various means, leading to a deeper understanding of him and his will. Axial coding identified 261 comments related to this category, which were grouped into four themes: God's Intervention, Receiving Enlightenment and Knowledge of God, Facing Challenges and Longing for Transformation, and Repentance for Spiritual Renewal. Table 11 provides an overview of the themes and subthemes within this category.

God's Intervention

Twenty participants shared experiences of how God intervened in their lives. Axial coding identified 86 related comments, which were categorized into three groups: Scripture and Praying, The Work of the Holy Spirit, and Other Means of Encountering God.

Scripture and Praying

Fifteen participants described how they gained a deeper understanding of God, his will, and his perspective through reading, meditating, and memorizing Scripture, as well as through prayer, fasting, and listening to sermons. Participant KF reflected on how reading the Psalms helped her shift from self-reliance in ministry to trusting in God:

> I had a strong desire to be recognized by other people ... I was also greedy about my ministry. But God has been changing me in these areas through his Word ... Ps 131:1–2 says, 'My heart is not proud, O LORD, my eyes are not haughty; I do not concern myself with great matters or things too wonderful for me. But I have stilled and quieted my soul, like a weaned child with its mother.' And 'Cast your cares of tomorrow to him!' I obeyed these Words, and the greed was gone. It was very simple. It is not a huge thing we are talking about. I went on expecting God's grace each and every day.[117]

Listening to sermons also became a means of transformation. One participant, who previously sought affirmation from a church leader, discovered her identity in Christ. She explained that she was able to understand who she is in Christ Jesus while she was listening to a sermon on the Internet:

> I had a fear of challenging new things ... By listening to the short sermons of Pastor David Wilkerson, I was able to understand who I am and how dearly God loves me ... He influenced me a lot ... I used to prioritize my pastor over God. That is why I once asked him not to abandon me. But as I got to know God, I realized that Jesus paid the price for me because he dearly loved me. Since then, my priorities changed ... [God became my top priority].[118]

Another participant experienced God's intervention through fasting and prayer during a period of financial distress:

> All financial support stopped ... At that moment, I didn't even have the strength to fast. I felt like dying ... For one month, I prayed, crying. I sent my prayer request to other intercessors. I wrestled in prayer. One thing I do well is fasting. Previously, the LORD answered my fasting, sometimes within several hours or a

---

117. KF, Transcript, 6–8.
118. AF, Transcript, 11–12.

few days. But this time, it didn't work that way. Between the first and third months, I started regaining confidence . . . After three months of prayer, I said to myself, 'I do not have to let others know of my dire situation because God will provide.'[119]

Participant SF said that she gained God's promise over the matter of her husband's salvation while reading the Word of God:

> I became anxious about my husband's salvation . . . God said to me to believe in him and his Word: 'Believe in the LORD Jesus, and you will be saved—you and your household.' I thanked God for giving me this Word and said, 'Truly, God is the one who does it, not me. God fulfills [his Word].' [Were you praying with the Word?] Yes, of course.[120]

The Work of the Holy Spirit

Thirteen participants described experiencing the Holy Spirit's intervention in various ways, such as hearing God's voice, receiving visions, sensing impressions, and experiencing inner and physical healing. For instance, Participant JF described hearing God's voice in the midst of relational difficulties:

> I said to myself, 'I am not the kind of person they think I am.' After the team left me, God started speaking to me, crying with me. He spoke to my heart and said, 'If you do not overcome this, you can't make it all the way [with me].' Then I asked, 'What should I do, LORD?' I decided to go back to the team and returned to them.[121]

A vision provided Participant QF with a powerful realization about God's presence, even among those she struggled to accept:

> We have lips that condemn and criticize people. One day, when a defector brother whom people didn't like came [to the meeting], I also didn't like him. I got angry . . . Suddenly, I saw Jesus standing behind him. I was startled . . . Since then, whenever I felt like criticizing or getting angry at someone, I called out the name of Jesus . . . It was not their problem but my problem of anger . . . The

---

119. MF, Transcript, 9.
120. SF, Transcript, 12.
121. JF, Transcript, 7.

reason I was angry at those people was because I lacked understanding and love for them.¹²²

Participant KF, who struggled with a tendency to criticize others, experienced the Holy Spirit's prompting to stop. She was also reminded of God's Word from Proverbs and, through meditation, gained strength from it:

> While I was worshiping, I caught myself criticizing the pastor and some people there. At that moment, I told myself to 'stop!' . . . I'm still not 100 percent changed . . . But the difference now is that I catch it right away, which is solely by God's grace. He tells me, 'You are condemning people!' . . . I don't know how many times I meditated on Prov 26:22: 'The words of a gossip are like choice morsels; they go down to a man's inmost parts.'¹²³

Participant KF also experienced the ministry of the Holy Spirit, receiving an inner healing from bitterness, pain, and anger, which might have been related to her habit of criticism during a spiritual conference she attended:

> How I longed to worship with [South Korean] believers? . . . But I was shocked when I saw deaconesses who had just worshiped with tears turn around and start criticizing and judging others . . . They even criticized me, both in my presence and absence, even though they didn't know me well. I decided to create my own system—layers of people who had different levels of access to my heart . . . However, one day as I was praying in tongues, the LORD helped me understand that the church is made up of people who confess that they are sinners . . . It was during a mission conference that the LORD began touching and healing my bitterness, pain, and anger.¹²⁴

Participant PF shared how she constantly senses God's presence, which helps her remain cautious about sin:

> Now I have a new Master. He has helped me since I was born in North Korea. Even now, in South Korea, he helps me . . . When your thoughts change, the world around you change . . . I have been enlightened to read the Bible . . . When I pray before his invisible presence, things happen in reality . . . I always feel that I live in his invisible presence, so I am never truly free . . . He is

---

122. QF, Transcript, 6.
123. KF, Transcript, 5.
124. KF, Transcript, 6.

watching me all the time ... I am cautious in my relationships with others ... He is a living God.[125]

Other Means of Encountering God

Three participants described how they gained spiritual insight through experiences such as hardship, hearing the lyrics of a song, or reflecting on their earthly fathers. One of them, facing conflict with a team, was reminded of a song lyric during a time of worship, which prompted her to seek reconciliation:

> While I was worshiping at the missionary's house [after I had a conflict with the team], I repented of my sin. Suddenly, the lyrics of a song I knew came to my mind: 'Why don't you approach first?' I almost died that day [from misery]. I went to the team leader and apologized for my actions. Later, I ran into the deaconesses who had criticized me. I threw my arms around them and asked for forgiveness.[126]

Another individual, identified here as RF, gained a deeper understanding of God's love reflecting on the kindness of her earthly father back in North Korea:

> God is my strength, my Rock, and my LORD ... He is my Father. He is just like my father back in North Korea ... He had six daughters and used to inquire after their friends, asking, 'How come that friend is not visiting our house recently?' I thought that all fathers were like mine, but I learned that was not the case ... God was saying to me, 'I made you, and I know you!' He is so kind and attentive. [I felt as if he was asking me], 'Are you going through a difficult time?' When I go through struggles, I sometimes complain to him, saying, 'You call me your daughter, but how long are you going to just watch me suffer?' My prayers are free like this ... At night, I tell him, 'Oh, Father! I was busy today. Thank you for giving me a comfortable and warm house [so I can rest].' 'While I sleep, please sit by me and watch over me.'[127]

---

125. PF, Transcript, 11.
126. JF, Transcript, 8.
127. RF, Transcript, 6.

This section examined how participants gained spiritual insight and understanding through various ways God intervened—through Scripture and prayer, the work of the Holy Spirit, and other means. While the Holy Spirit can move at any time, the findings suggest that he often speaks when individuals position themselves in worship, meditation on Scripture, and prayer with an attentive spirit. The next section will explore the specific insights participants gained through these encounters with God.

Receiving Enlightenment and Knowledge of God

All 20 participants spoke of receiving spiritual knowledge of God, which contributed significantly to the transformation of their worldview. Axial coding identified 76 related comments, categorized into three subthemes: Revelatory Insights, Corrections, and Guidance.

Revelatory Insights

Fourteen participants described how God revealed aspects of his nature and their own identity through his intervention. They came to understand God as loving, faithful, living, eternal, healing, and forgiving. Additionally, they gained a renewed sense of self-identity as God's servants and children of the King. Participant AF shared how reading the Bible gave her a new perspective on finances during a difficult time when she struggled to send remittances to her relatives in North Korea:

> At one point, I really struggled with financial difficulties . . . I had my grandmom and an uncle who raised me back in the North. I wanted to help them, but there seemed no way. I tried to quit the Bible school I was in . . . However, I was reading the Bible, Prov 30:7–9: 'Two things I ask of you, O LORD . . . give me neither poverty nor riches, but give me only my daily bread. Otherwise, I may have too much and disown you . . . or I may become poor and steal.' After reading it, I realized that I lost my first intention. I said to God, . . . 'Why and how did I come all the way here?' I came because I was hungry . . . My heart and intention had changed . . . Money came first . . . I was just in a hurry to send money to the North without praying and without consulting with the pastor . . . I tried to quit school. But the Word upheld and restored my heart. I prayed that the LORD wouldn't allow me to become a slave of

money . . . I came to believe that when there is a need, God will surely take care of me.[128]

Participant AF shared how reading the Bible gave her a new perspective on her purpose in life:

> After I met the LORD, I realized how precious and blessed I was [laugh]. I used to be sad because I had nothing. Even though I still don't have anything such as money or parents, the greatest One is with me, and I don't care much about anything else. Now my mind is renewed . . . The Bible says, 'So whether you eat or drink or whatever you do, do it all for the glory of God.' I realized that I am to live for God's glory . . . I think a lot about the ways that I can give glory to him in my preparation to enter college.[129]

Corrections

Fifteen participants spoke of how God intervened in their lives to correct their misconceptions and attitudes and convict them of areas where they had strayed. Examples of these instances include being critical of others or prioritizing personal concerns over his kingdom. Participant BF described how her perspective shifted from idolizing her son to entrusting him to God in prayer:

> My son was my idol always. He was the standard [of my life]. However, the Word says that I can't make an idol, and my son can't be the idol. God should come first. The missionaries here teach, and the Word says the same thing—that I should let down my son. As I was reading the Bible, I realized that there is nothing I can do about my son, even though I have my own ideas and thoughts. I cannot even implement those things. Then, I thought I should let him down and pray to God.[130]

Participant MF shared how God changed her heart, moving her from despair to trust in him:

> Previously, I even thought about committing suicide. [During the prayer] The LORD reminded me of my time in China when I met the LORD in the wilderness . . . Surely, I gained strength.

128. AF, Transcript, 12.
129. AF, Transcript, 6, 11.
130. BF, Transcript, 5.

> After three months of prayer, I said to myself, 'I do not have to let others know of my dire situation because God will provide.' God sees everything! I was completely changed. The condition of my heart . . . What was inside of me was all disclosed, but now it was changed into confidence. 'This ministry is God's. Why should I worry about it?'[131]

Guidance

Five participants shared how they gained a deeper understanding of God through his guidance. Participant LF described how God's Word led her to remain silent as a means of victory when she faced accusations:

> When I do YouTube broadcasting [and encounter unexpected responses from some people], I get to think that the person might be a non-Christian. Then, I feel much lighter, thinking that his/her worldview is quite different from a Christian one. However, when it is a Christian, I feel so bothered. How can a Christian think like that? . . . Sometimes, even when I talk about loving an enemy, they seem to have a problem with it . . . The Bible says that Jesus acquired victory by being crucified without saying anything. I know how to win. Sometimes silence without disclosing every detail can bring me victory . . . I meditate on Jesus' ways. When the right time comes, I think that the LORD will reveal everything which was not possible with me in the past.'[132]

The participants' experiences of God's intervening presence contributed to growth in their understanding of God, his will, and perspectives. Specifically, their testimonies illustrate the diverse ways in which participants received knowledge of God through revelation, correction, or guidance. All of these ways of engaging with God contributed to their worldview transformation.

Facing Challenges and Longing for Transformation

Eighteen participants made comments about facing challenges and/or longings for spiritual transformation. The axial coding shows 53 comments that are grouped into four subthemes: Inner Struggles for Sanctification,

---

131. MF, Transcript, 9.
132. LF, Transcript, 7.

FINDINGS

Seeking God's Kingdom and Perspectives, and Desiring a Deeper Relationship with God.

Inner Struggles for Sanctification

Spiritual growth often involves inner struggles as believers confront their weaknesses and seek transformation. For some, this means overcoming ingrained attitudes and emotions, while for others, it requires surrendering their own efforts and desires to God. These accounts reveal the participants' struggles with self-will, emotional burdens, and reliance on their own strength. Through these challenges of sanctification, they came to understand that true transformation occurs when they surrender to God's ways rather than depend on themselves.

Specifically, 11 participants shared how their growing understanding of God, his will, and his purpose led them to wrestle with personal sanctification, expressing a deep longing to reflect Christ more fully in their lives. Participant FM described his struggle with criticism and resentment, recognizing the need to change his attitude to resemble Christ in order to serve others effectively:

> I still have lots of problems in the area of human relationships . . . I put down my spoon in the midst of eating whenever I think of the xx politician. I struggle with this attitude because I am a servant of God. It would be difficult to save others unless I change . . . I get to meditate on the life of Jesus . . . Jesus used to get angry too, but I shouldn't turn to the left nor the right but remain in the lifestyle of Jesus Christ as a harmonizing servant, saint, and worker so that I can confidently handle the defectors who are tough.[133]

For Participant AF, experiencing God's intervention in a time of distress led to a renewed desire to seek him above all else:

> He said that he is with me and the world. I want him more . . . Sometimes I pray for what I want . . . However, I want to change my prayers [from now on]. I want my life to desire God more and die to myself more.[134]

---

133. DM, Transcript, 7.
134. AF, Transcript, 11.

Participant HM shared how a moment of divine confrontation in the concentration camp in North Korea made him realize his reliance on human strength rather than fully depending on God:

> I was shocked! [He heard God saying, 'You tried to fulfill the promise that I made with you with your own strength! You have to do it with me! And you need to obey my Word.'] I looked back on my life . . . Even though I said that I trusted God, I realized that I had trusted men instead.[135]

Seeking God's Kingdom and Perspective

Nine participants spoke about the challenges and longings they experienced in seeking God's kingdom and understanding his perspective. Their testimonies reflected a desire to engage in evangelism, foster unity in the body of Christ, and gain deeper insight into God's will and plan for their lives. Participant PF shared how the Holy Spirit delivered her from worries and feelings of low self-worth, leading her to realize that she was called to live for God's kingdom:

> I said to myself, 'Now that the LORD gave me life, I need to work for him. All I could do is to share the gospel.' So, I found a reason to live![136]

Participant GF explained how understanding the body of Christ through Scripture gave her a vision to embrace Israel and other nations in unity under Christ:

> In the visions, God shared his Word with me from John 17, which was his priestly prayer to the Father before his crucifixion. The prayer centered around love and the desire for unity. It is also related to the passage in Malachi 4 that speaks of being united as one, where the Father's heart turns toward the children, and the children's hearts turn toward the Father. My mentor consistently emphasized the importance of loving one another and becoming a unified body, like a bride preparing for Jesus. This unity is crucial for the restoration of the highway mentioned in Isaiah 19. As Christians, we are all part of one family.[137]

---

135. HM, Transcript, 9.
136. PF, Transcript, 7.
137. GF, Transcript, 6.

Findings

Desiring a Deeper Relationship with God

Eight participants expressed a desire for a deeper relationship with God, even as they faced challenges that tested their faith. Their testimonies reflect a longing to know God more intimately and to overcome personal barriers in their spiritual journey. Participant AF shared how her longing for God grew as she prioritized him above all else:

> He is with me and the world. I have a desire to pursue God more and give him priority over all other things. When I listen to his sermon, my thoughts and desires change significantly.[138]

Participant SF confessed that she initially saw God as distant and stern, which made it difficult for her to understand how to love him:

> [She confessed to God,] 'God, I want to love You. However, I do not know how to love You.' To me, he was a fearful God who rebuked and turned his face from me whenever I made a mistake, just like my strict father and mother. I could not sense God's tender care or his deep love for me at all. While I was praying like this, he visited me and revealed what was inside of me.[139]

Participant IM also expressed his yearnings to grow closer to God, seeking:

> I long for a relationship with God . . . I felt like I was bound by a system.[140]

In summary, more than half of the participants testified to their struggles and desires for sanctification as they sought a deeper relationship with God. Nearly half also faced challenges while longing to understand God's will and kingdom perspective, particularly in relation to their ministries. Some wrestled with personal attitudes and self-reliance, recognizing their need to trust in God's strength, step out of their comfort zones, and fully surrender to him. The following section will examine the theme, Coming to Repentance.

---

138. AF, Transcript, 11.
139. SF, Transcript, 3.
140. IM, Transcript, 19.

Repentance for Spiritual Renewal

Eighteen participants commented on repenting of their sins after receiving enlightenment and knowledge of God and his will. Axial coding identified 38 comments, categorized into four groups: Resistance to God's Lordship, Immorality and Spiritual Negligence, Self-Reliance and Self-Righteousness, and Anger, Bitterness, and Hatred.

Resistance to God's Lordship

Ten participants repented of their resistance to God's lordship, which involved criticism, insisting on their own way, lack of trust in God, and idol worship. Participant SF described how she repented of her pride after hearing from God:

> I am not an ordinary North Korean defector but special . . . My father fought for your lives with his life, but what were you doing then?' Also, I am a daughter of God who lays down my life every day to preach the gospel. However, if I were to remain in this group, they wouldn't let me be alone, accusing me of being a pastor with Juche ideology . . . I said to myself, 'I am not the kind of person that you think.' After the team left me, God started speaking to me, crying with me. God spoke to my heart and said, 'If you do not overcome this, you can't make it all the way [with Me].' Then I said, 'What should I do, LORD?' I said I would go back to the team and returned to them.[141]

Participant MF, convicted of her tendency to enforce blind obedience on her children and congregation, repented and committed herself to serious training in Scripture and prayer:

> I had a framework of absolute obedience [just like in North Korea]. According to God's Word, obedience happens when a person is given faith to do it. It is quite different from [blind] obedience that I demand from people. It is more like my desire, and it comes from my personality, which is something I need to repent of . . . [How did it go after the conviction?] Now, I am in intensive training in reading the Word and prayer . . . I spend most of my time in prayer and reading spiritual books . . . Whatever I see, I try to see it from God's perspective . . . I say, 'Ah, this is wrong from God's perspective, and that is what God is pleased with!' I also try to

---

141. JF, Transcript, 7–8.

discern my position in God in regard to my ministry, actions, and words ... I continue to wrestle with God's Word.[142]

Participant TM, convicted of his complacency in enjoying a comfortable life while neglecting his calling to North Korean missions, repented and took action:

> The finger was enlarged and flew into my heart and got stuck. It was like a knife stabbing my heart. I said, 'I can't live like this anymore.' I repented of my sin and was revived as I worshiped God with my family that very night ... I quit my job and withdrew all my money to join DTS.[143]

Immorality and Spiritual Negligence

Five participants repented of sins related to immorality and spiritual negligence, including sexual impurity, violence, dishonesty, malicious speech, careless living, and neglect of spiritual training. Participant EF described how the Holy Spirit revealed her past theft like a film as she prayed:

> Lying in North Korea didn't matter as long as I could survive. I borrowed money from my friend using lies ... I felt no guilt when I stole from someone's field as long as I didn't get caught [laughing]. I used to have no shame, but now I feel guilty even when I glance at someone's writing without permission ... [How did that happen?] It was God's Word. God's Word became my standard. [The Bible says,] 'Do not steal. Do not murder.' Whenever needed, God's Word touches my conscience.[144]

Participant QF repented of her negligence in spiritual training when the Holy Spirit convicted her of its importance:

> I quit for one semester [of the prayer school], but I repented deeply when I understood that it was not just a school. It was a training program for God's army. Since then, I have not missed a single semester [at the prayer school of xx mission agency]. Even though I hear the same lectures repeatedly, every time, something convicts me about areas of my life that need change.[145]

142. MF, Transcript, 7.
143. TM, Transcript, 7.
144. EF, Transcript, 16.
145. QF, Transcript, 8.

Self-Reliance and Self-Righteousness

Four participants repented of their self-reliance and self-righteousness. Participant SF recounted her struggle with self-righteousness, realizing that she had placed her sense of identity in her own integrity and moral conduct rather than in God's grace:

> I used to think that my integrity and righteous life defined my identity... However, when the LORD shone his searchlight into my heart, I saw my own hypocrisy... If I were truly honest, I shouldn't have eaten the food my husband brought home. His sole purpose was to provide for his wife and children, no matter what he did—including stealing from others... I used to despise him for harming others... My husband doesn't even eat the food he brings home, but he feels happy when his wife and children eat it joyfully... I was the one who made others bleed using my husband's hands.[146]

Anger, Bitterness, and Hatred

Four participants came to recognize that repentance is a continual process in the Christian life as they identified anger, bitterness, and hatred as obstacles to spiritual renewal. Among them, Participant JF relayed that she had had to repent of her resentment toward South Korean ministers, whom she had perceived as underestimating the success of the North Korean defector ministry:

> The North Korean defector ministry [I led] was experiencing a revival. However, it was looked down upon and dismissed as insignificant [by South Korean ministers]. I felt angry when I was alone. Sometimes, I would call my friend and start cursing them out of frustration... I don't get angry at North Koreans but only at South Koreans.[147]

This subsection has outlined the theme of Repentance for Spiritual Renewal. As participants grew in their understanding of God, his will, and his perspective through experiencing his presence, they were led to repentance. This process served to remove the hindrances that obstructed their transformation into a Christian worldview.

146. SF, Transcript, 4.
147. JF, Transcript, 5.

Findings

Returning to the overarching theme of *Growth in Understanding of God, His Will, and His Perspective* (Table 11), the collected data have been categorized into four key themes: God's Intervention, Receiving Enlightenment and Knowledge of God, Facing Challenges and Longing for Transformation, and Repentance for Spiritual Renewal. The interview contents reveal that God revealed his presence through Scripture and prayer to the participants, and the work of the Holy Spirit deepened their knowledge of God. For some, this led to repentance, while others developed a longing for a closer relationship with God. The findings suggest that God's purpose in this process was to draw participants into deeper communion with him—removing the sin that hindered their relationship with him and awakening in them a greater desire for his presence. The next section will examine the category of *Experiencing God*.

Experiencing God

This section presents participants' reflections on their experiences of God based on responses to the fifth and sixth questions in the questionnaire. Axial coding identified 149 relevant comments, which were categorized into four overarching themes: Internalization of God's Word, Experiencing God through the Word, Divinely Bestowed Emotions, and Evidence of Transformation. Table 12 below provides an overview of these themes and their corresponding subthemes.

Table 12. Theme and Subthemes of Experiencing God
(P: number of participants; C: number of comments)

Category	Themes and Subthemes	P	C
Experiencing God	*Internalization of God's Word*	20	59
	Persevering in Prayers	17	39
	Studying and Meditating on Scripture	7	12
	Maintaining a Daily Devotional Time	5	8
	Experiencing God through the Word	18	45
	Perceiving God's Nature	14	37
	Gaining Insight into God's Name	7	8
	Divinely Bestowed Emotions (Love, Joy, Freedom, Confidence, and Fearlessness)	17	28
	Evidence of Transformation	8	21

Internalization of God's Word

Twenty participants highlighted the importance of persistently engaging with Scripture through prayer, meditation, and a daily devotional time to allow God's Word to transform their lives. They recognized that internalizing God's Word required continuous effort to align their thoughts, beliefs, and actions with biblical truth. Axial coding revealed four main themes: Persevering in Prayer, Studying and Meditating on Scripture, and Maintaining a Daily Devotional Time.

Persevering in Prayers

Seventeen participants emphasized the importance of persevering in prayer for the internalization of God's Word. Participant KF described her ongoing struggle in this process, relying on persistent prayer and a conscious effort to align her will with God's Word:

> I realized that even after I met the LORD in a personal way, my old habits and personality kept pulling me back to where I used to be. Only when I surrendered my will to God and sought his presence for help was I able to overcome the problem. According to the personal enlightenment I received, I now try to speak as little as possible by keeping my mouth in check.[148]

Participant SF shared wrestling with God in the area of self-righteousness. Through this process, she came to a profound realization that her self-righteousness was, in reality, a form of rebellion against him. This revelation led her to persevere in prayer, seeking to align her heart with God's Word. Her ultimate goal was for God's truth to shape her beliefs and guide her actions:

> I had no choice but to prepare a table of alcoholic drinks and snacks for my husband and the defectors he invited to our house. It was a challenging and difficult time for me, and I felt like I was in a spiritual battle. I prayed fervently for each of them, longing to see a transformation in their lives. There were moments when I saw changes, but the process seemed never-ending, like going through a tunnel with no end in sight. I became exhausted and questioned what God was doing in the midst of it all . . . I reached a point where I wanted to give up and let everything go. I fell into a

---

148. KF, Transcript, 5.

state of depression . . . It seemed like there was no word from God and, more importantly, no noticeable change in the situation. Yet in the midst of this struggle, God revealed the depths of my own brokenness and shortcomings. He showed me that my attempts at righteousness were actually acts of rebellion against him.[149]
[What was the biggest factor that caused the worldview change?] The biggest factor that led to my worldview change was the intersection of God's Word and my life . . . It was only through God's grace that the Word of life became truly embedded in me . . . This grace came alongside my persistent prayers . . . Because God's Word is far greater and limitless compared to my current reality, it continually calls me to [a higher place].[150]

Similarly, Participant OM described his need for persevering prayer to fulfill God's command to love anyone he placed in his life, even those who were difficult to embrace:

> Even in the midst of experiencing God's grace, when I saw a certain person, I felt bad and uncomfortable . . . I can say that the difference between believers and non-believers is this: even though it is painful for me to just watch the person, I try to embrace him and change through prayer . . . Obedience, prayer, and trying to see from a different perspective . . . Non-believers give up easily and run away.[151]

For Participant BF, experiencing continuous answers to prayer became a source of motivation, deepening her understanding of God's nature and affirming his presence in her life:

> I told myself that I needed to pray! God answers all my prayers . . . Through this process, I came to understand so much and cried out, saying, 'Truly, God exists, and he is living!' After I met the LORD, I received many answered prayers—not necessarily for big things, but even for the small matters in my life. I don't do anything without praying first, and then things go smoothly. Even for the simplest things that people normally do without thinking, I pray before acting. Again, God answers my prayers.[152]

---

149. SF, Transcript, 9–10.
150. SF, Transcript, 14.
151. OM, Transcript, 6.
152. AF, Transcript, 1.

Participant EF described how God penetrated her heart, breaking down her ego and shifting her focus away from worldly desires. She shared that through perseverance and a determined focus on the kingdom of God, she experienced a transformative process. As a result, she began to witness the fulfillment of God's promise, "Seek first his kingdom and his righteousness, and all these things will be given to you as well":

> My value system . . . the purpose of my life . . . all changed. I had nothing to envy anymore. God provided me with more than enough . . . The process was this: God broke my ego. In other words, he was working in my heart to make me die to myself so that he could work through me . . . However, my ego was strong, leading me to resist God's work of breaking me . . . For example, I always prayed for a pure and clean spirit . . . I wanted to be honest at all times . . . Yet, I saw myself giving in to temptations . . . So many things like that happened [where God revealed what was inside of me]. This process allowed me to recognize my own limitations, leading to a deeper reliance on God's strength rather than my own.[153]

Studying and Meditating on Scripture (Reading, Meditating, and Memorizing)

Seven participants commented on their practice of training in the Word as part of the internalization process of God's Word. However, they emphasized that this was inseparable from approaching God persistently in prayer. Participant LF shared how meditating on God's love, as demonstrated through Jesus' sacrifice on the cross, deeply impacted her. She described how her dedicated reflection on this truth led to a profound experience of unity with Christ:

> When we look up at the cross from below, we see two hands nailed, along with the feet . . . I asked, 'Could this be the worst physical pain a person can endure?' But when the body suffers, the soul suffers as well . . . No matter what, I wondered, how much must he have loved me to die for me? I thought about it deeply . . . The many experiences of God's love have become condensed within me. Based on how much I have experienced his love . . . When the LORD sees something from his perspective, if we can see it the same way, we not only understand but also feel what he feels . . . This is

---

153. EF, Transcript, 11–12.

not something that can be grasped by intellectual understanding alone—it goes beyond that into a deep sense of unity with him . . . 'Can we truly love our enemies if we only understand the concept in our minds?' Just standing beneath the cross and acknowledging that he died for me is not enough to enable us to forgive our enemies. It has to become personal—my own experience. When I am united with Christ's love for me, when I experience it both physically and spiritually, identification takes place. Then, it is no longer 'I' who forgives, but forgiveness becomes possible through him.[154]

She further reflected on how experiencing the Holy Spirit through God's Word created lasting transformation rather than a fleeting intellectual realization:

As long as I remain in a relationship with the LORD, his Word—whether through hearing, reading, or meditating—along with experiences of the Holy Spirit and prayer, continues to shape me . . . When I am enlightened by God's truth, there may be many inspiring writings that make me think, 'Oh, I should live like that!' However, such realizations remain superficial and do not become embodied in my life. But when an experience of the Holy Spirit or God's Word simultaneously touches my spirit and takes hold of me, it becomes deeply rooted within me. When that happens, power is generated from within to overcome [difficulties].[155]

Participant KF, recognizing her struggle with a critical spirit, described how she disciplined herself to counter this tendency by meditating on Scripture:

We are created in God's image, and our words carry power. The Bible speaks extensively about the words we speak. This has always been my greatest weakness, and likely that of many defectors—criticism and condemnation! We were raised in an environment that encouraged this . . . Whenever I feel the urge to criticize and begin feeling uneasy, I turn to meditation on God's Word, starting from Genesis . . . I reflect on Adam and continue all the way to Jesus. By the time I complete my meditation, the temptation to criticize is gone.[156]

---

154. LF, Transcript, 6–7.
155. LF, Transcript, 8.
156. KF, Transcript, 5.

Likewise, Participant CF described how her perspective toward others changed as she meditated on Christ's sacrifice and love:

> I used to hate and speak harshly about people who were mean to me. But now, that is changing. Whenever I think of Jesus Christ dying on the cross for someone as unworthy as me, I cannot dare to hate another person. Even if I do criticize or condemn someone, I feel convicted of my sin immediately and repent. This has been a significant change in my life.[157]

Maintaining a Daily Devotional Time

Five participants emphasized the crucial role of maintaining a daily devotional time for the internalization of God's Word, highlighting its deep connection to consistent training in the Word and unwavering perseverance in prayer. On his first day of imprisonment in a North Korean concentration camp, Participant HM repented when God revealed his reliance on self-accomplishment and trust in men rather than in him. This realization shook him, compelling him to devote himself to daily Bible reading and prayer in his prison cell:

> I reflected on my life at that time and came to realize that I had been relying on my own ways and putting my trust in people. God spoke to me, urging me to obey him and to do things in partnership with him. In response, I immediately began engaging in daily prayers and reading the Bible. I sought the LORD wholeheartedly in my prison cell. Surprisingly, my time in prison proved to be spiritually transformative. I came to understand that God was watching over me and guiding me with his love and grace. The most significant change within me was a newfound assurance of his love and kindness, particularly in relation to my faith in God.[158]

Participant AF made it a priority to devote her time to God, recognizing its utmost importance in her life. As she gained a deeper understanding of God's love for her, she began to rely less on other people for fulfillment and support:

> I used to rely on people . . . However, I came to the realization that my friends should not be my primary focus. There were times

---

157. CF, Transcript, 4.
158. HM, Transcript, 4, 9.

when I neglected my time with God, and it dawned on me that I needed to prioritize my relationship with him. I recognized the importance of securing dedicated time to be in his presence and engage in prayer. Through this process, I began to experience significant changes in my life. As I grew in my understanding of God's love for me and the sacrifice he made, my perspectives and priorities underwent a transformation. I became aware that my previous priorities were misguided, [and I embraced a new perspective centered on God and his love for me].[159]

This section of the analysis highlights that internalizing God's Word takes time and requires perseverance in prayer, as the participants testified. As Participant SF noted, our reality often feels far from God's perfect will. However, the more we approach God with open hearts in prayer, the more deeply his Word penetrates our spirit until we become one with it. In other words, when the time is right, God takes hold of our spirit through his Word and rules within us. This transformation is often evident to those around us, as seen in the experiences of the eight participants who underwent a genuine shift toward a biblical worldview, which will be discussed later in this chapter. Throughout this process, the participants frequently encountered God's nature through his Word, experiencing and expressing the imparted emotions of love, joy, and peace.

Experiencing God through the Word

Eighteen participants described experiencing God through the Word. Axial coding identified 45 related comments, which were grouped into two subthemes: Perceiving God's Nature and Gaining Insight into God's Name.

Perceiving God's Nature

Fourteen participants shared their experiences of encountering God through various aspects of his nature as revealed in Scripture. They described him as one who loves, cares, helps, leads, guides, calls, and answers prayer. They also experienced God as ever-present, a source of healing, refreshment, and provision. While these experiences reflected different aspects of God's nature, they all centered on the overarching theme of his love. It was because of this deep love that God intervened in their lives in

159. AF, Transcript, 11–12.

such profound ways. Participant NM recounted how he was overwhelmed by God's immense love when God touched his broken heart, marking a turning point in his life:

> 'What would you do, God, about the children who died? Please give me some understanding,' I shouted from the top of the rock at the seashore. In that moment, I truly grasped the profound meaning of the righteous living by faith. As an evangelical, I had never been particularly drawn to visions, dreams, or the gifts of the Holy Spirit. However, it was not exactly a vision but rather a deep awareness that he was opening my spiritual eyes. My attitude immediately changed when God revealed his immense love for us. God said, 'You don't have to feel pain [for the dead children] because it is something that I take care of. You felt the pain, but did you ever pray about it?' He also reminded me of the tears I shed while watching the Jesus movie in China, saying, 'It was me!' It does not matter how strong a person may be; in the face of such love on the cross, they will crumble. His love struck me so powerfully that my body was drenched in sweat. For the next few hours, memories of my past flashed through my mind like a film. Even in that train accident, I did not die—God had always been with me, though I had not realized it. Moreover, I finally understood that in the kingdom of God, he had already welcomed the children who died, and perhaps it was better for them to be with him early rather than perish from consuming harmful substances on the streets. He renewed my calling for North Korea.[160]

Participant TM described how he was freed from fear, insecurity, unforgiveness, and distorted, unbiblical views of God when he heard God's voice saying, "I love you!":

> He said to me, 'I love you!' Before that, he was a God I feared. I first encountered the LORD in a miraculous way, but I believed that unless I did something for him, I would be punished. Fear consumed me constantly, even while working at the company. But at that moment, God spoke to me, saying, 'I am the God who does not punish you but loves you just as you are . . . whether you were in North Korea, working at the company, or now—I love you as you are! That is why Jesus Christ died for you on the cross.' From that point on, my life was completely transformed. I used to be

---

160. NM, Transcript, 6.

Findings

critical and judgmental of others, but now I have become loving and forgiving. Even my perception of myself has changed.[161]

Participant QF shared how her daily devotional time in God's Word brought renewal and freed her from the grudge she held against her husband:

> Every day, God gives me his Word in a way that speaks to my circumstances and brings restoration to my life. When the LORD opened my spiritual eyes to see my husband's heart, I realized he was not a bad person. Through this revelation, the issue was finally resolved.[162]

Participant RF shared that the greatest transformation in her life came through immersing herself in God's Word, as God poured his love into her heart, filling her with gratitude and enabling her to share his love with others:

> The greatest transformation in my life came through immersing myself in God's Word. He poured his love into my heart, and I am deeply grateful for his guidance throughout my life. This gratitude naturally overflows to those around me. Love is patient and chooses to see beyond the flaws of others. I am thankful for the gift of life and always hold in my heart the truth that I am a woman of God. Our lives themselves serve as testimony and an example to others. Through me, God's gentleness, gratitude, patience, and faithfulness are revealed.[163]

Participant GF shared her experience of physical healing as God spoke a prophetic word to her about the unity of South and North Korea:

> I suffered from epilepsy as a result of the torture I endured in North Korea. To cope, I depended on sleeping pills. When I arrived in Israel at night, I took my medication and went to sleep. The next morning, I had to attend a conference, but I still felt groggy and disoriented. As I entered the hall, I saw Jewish Christians and Palestinian Christians holding hands and praying together. At that moment, I stood frozen. Suddenly, a warm sensation washed over me from head to toe, and I heard God's voice saying, 'The same thing is going to happen in Korea!' From that day on, I no longer needed sleeping pills. Remarkably, I became a more optimistic person. My body was healed, and my mind became clear, which

---

161. TM, Transcript, 11–12.
162. QF, Transcript, 10.
163. RF, Transcript, 9.

astonished my husband. He had to acknowledge that God truly is alive![164]

Additionally, Participant GF encountered God's Word, guiding and calling her as she endured a forced abortion in North Korea:

> I plunged into a state of panic as my unborn baby was mercilessly torn from me. The agony brought to mind the image of Jesus on the cross, as depicted in the movie I watched while in China. When people see it, they all recognize the unbearable pain he endured—his crucifixion, his scourging, and the piercing of his hands and feet. Yet, in that moment, God revealed his heart to me—the heart of a Father who could only watch as his Son was crucified, whipped, and nailed. It was overwhelming. I love my two daughters dearly and would never allow anyone to harm or mistreat them. Yet God simply watched as his Son was beaten and put to death. There are no words to describe it fully. His heart poured out onto me.
>
> They performed the abortion without anesthesia, forcing me to endure unimaginable pain—pain no one should have to bear. But after hearing God's voice, I could only sympathize with him.[165]

By experiencing God's comfort and love, JF overcame her bitterness and interpersonal struggles:

> God said, 'My dear!' He wept with me and poured out his heart to me. I felt as though he was saying, 'If you don't overcome this situation, you won't be able to go all the way with me.' I asked, 'So what should I do? Should I go back to them?' Looking like an absolute beggar, I returned to them.[166]

Gaining Insight into God's Name

Seven participants described their experiences of God through the various ways he is addressed, such as LORD, Father, and the Way. While some of these experiences overlap with their encounters with God's love, as they also reflect his actions, Participant DM's story vividly illustrates how

---

164. GF, Transcript, 6–7.
165. GF, Transcript, 5.
166. JF, Transcript, 7.

encountering God in a way that revealed the true meaning of his biblical names transformed her life, enabling her to call on him by that very name:

> I prayed, 'God, I now understand the Way that mankind should follow. You are the Alpha and the Omega, and I have come to know your Way.' . . . Jesus said, 'I am the Way, the Truth, and the Life. No one comes to the Father except through me.' Therefore, neither communism nor capitalism is the answer—the true path is one of absolute devotion to God! I am determined to live by it. However, the challenge is that I am the only one who knows this Way. The people of Chosun [North Korea] must also come to know it. Therefore, the Bible must be translated into Korean so they can understand your Way as well . . . LORD, I will undertake this task![167]

While in prison, Participant OM came to know God as his LORD through the letters he received:

> They spoke of God's love and sovereignty. Around that time, I felt my heart gradually closing toward God, yet these letters continued to knock, preventing me from shutting it completely. Slowly, I realized that what I had believed to be right was, in fact, wrong. It was then that I had to renounce the self-righteousness that had sustained me throughout my 8 years of imprisonment. It felt as though my soul had left me. I understood that I desperately needed to seek the living and true God, which brought me great anguish. After some time, I had no choice but to confess that from that moment on, I must live solely in the LORD and according to his will, not my own![168]

When the empowering presence of the Holy Spirit came upon TM, he was emboldened and resolved to smuggle Bibles back into North Korea:

> Many pastors asked how I found the courage to return to North Korea with a backpack filled with 25 Bibles, a wooden cross (20cm x 40cm), and various Bible-related materials, fully aware of the risk of capture and execution. I told them it was not my own strength but God's power at work within me. I had come to understand the account in Acts 2, where the Holy Spirit descended upon 120 individuals, freeing them from fear and empowering them to proclaim the gospel. It was God who led me with his divine power.[169]

167. DM, Transcript, 4.
168. OM, Transcript, 5.
169. TM, Transcript, 8.

> As I stood at the border, just 500 meters from a State Security Agency soldier, I trembled inwardly, desperately crying out to God for help. Suddenly, a truck arrived, and the guard, recognizing the driver, stepped away from his post. At that moment, I knew that God had intervened to save me. With newfound boldness, I went on to share the gospel with my family and relatives in North Korea.[170]

During a prophetic vision about events in North Korea, QF encountered God as the Healer. She not only witnessed his revelation but also experienced his healing power firsthand when her chronically cold hands and feet were miraculously restored:

> On the third day of the conference, the LORD Jesus Christ appeared to me in the image of himself hanging on the cross. I broke into tears and repented for not embracing other defectors who carried the same pain in their hearts. Then, in spirit, he took me to North Korea. Everywhere I went, there was a bright light. I saw the concentration camps and prisons, but they were no more—the doors were open and filled with light. A profound peace washed over my heart, and I felt light. Suddenly, warmth spread through my body, reaching even my hands and feet. In the past, when people shook my hands at church, they would jokingly ask, 'Are you still alive?' because of how cold they were. But at that moment, my body was warm for the first time.[171]

As discerned from the data, when the participants encountered God, they were overwhelmed by his love, comfort, freedom from fear, and the confidence that comes from trusting him. They also gained a deeper understanding of their identities. Through his love, they came to see that God cared for them and that he truly loved them.

Divinely Bestowed Emotions

Through their encounters with God, participants often experienced emotions that he bestowed upon them. Seventeen participants described feeling love, joy, peace, freedom, fearlessness, and confidence as they experienced God, primarily through his Word. Participant SF reflected on this transformation:

---

170. TM, Transcript, 8–9.
171. QF, Transcript, 4–5.

> It didn't make sense that he died for me. However, when his love was poured into my heart, I found myself able to love effortlessly. If he loved me, someone filthier than a sewer, was there anyone I could not embrace or understand? God gave me something beyond my understanding.[172]

Participant NM recounted his experience of encountering God's love and the profound realization that transformed his unbiblical thoughts about God:

> He reminded me of the tears I shed while watching the Jesus movie in China. He said, 'It was me!' It didn't matter how strong a person might be—before such love on the cross, anyone would break . . . His love struck me powerfully!.[173]

Altogether, these testimonies reveal how experiencing God's love softened the hardened hearts of participants, enabling individuals like NM to return to the LORD after 8 years of distance caused by disappointment with him. Similarly, many participants who encountered God also experienced his love, which led them to express the emotions he imparted—love, joy, and peace.

Evidence of Transformation

Eight participants shared how those around them recognized the evidence of transformation in their lives, reflecting the likeness of Jesus Christ. Their testimonies also include instances where they responded immediately to God's Word, demonstrating full surrender to the lordship of Jesus Christ. These changes serve as signs of their transformation toward a biblical worldview. Some accounts highlight a life marked by love, personal breakthroughs in handling criticism, and a commitment to prioritizing God's will above all else. Participant LF recollected how she reconciled a broken friendship through enduring love, providing further testimony of transformation, and explained the factor that led to this change:

> What is being established in me . . . ironically, I come to know it by hearing what others say about me . . . Two years ago, I reconnected with a childhood friend who was not a believer. Last year, when something in our relationship made her uneasy, she suddenly cut

---

172. SF, Transcript, 4.
173. NM, Transcript, 6.

off communication . . . I didn't know what had gone wrong . . . I kept sending her text messages, and I believe God impressed upon my heart to tell her that I loved her and was waiting for her . . . If she had truly wanted to end our relationship, she could have blocked me. Instead, she read my messages but never responded . . . In that process, I reflected on God's heart—waiting in love even without receiving a response . . . I don't know if I ever had that kind of patience before . . . In the end, she and her husband came to see me and even paid 3 years' worth of overdue membership fees. Then, out of nowhere, she told me that my leadership was 'almost perfect' and admitted she had misunderstood me. She said, 'If it were anyone else, they would have given up on me, but you waited—for just one member of the group.' As I listened to her, I realized that I was changing.[174]

[What do you think was the factor that changed you?] It is God . . . In one word, his great love. The power of love seems to be the greatest force. However, as I mentioned earlier, love is not only strong—it is also warm. It is warm, but that warmth is not weakness. It is both warm and strong . . . Should I say that it has the power to change everything at the core? If this love reaches the world, souls will be saved—aren't we called to play a part in that? Then how can we fulfill that role? I have been thinking about this . . . Recently, I have often used the term 'channel.' There was a case involving a member of our cooperative whose mother contracted COVID-19 and needed a lung transplant while receiving basic living support. We are channels of God's love to others—channels of blessing, channels of rescue . . . Looking back on my life, what truly matters to me is rescuing people . . . That has become my focus . . . In the end, from the power of love comes the power of forgiveness . . . It is not just about loving one's enemies. The ability to overcome the difficulties in my life depends on the depth of love within me.[175]

After returning to the LORD after 8 years of distance from his faith, Participant NM experienced a renewed sense of God's love. This rekindled connection with God led him to promptly enroll in seminary, pursuing the calling he had received long ago. Those around him witnessed the transformation in his life as follows:

There was a sister at church whom I had fought with. I hated her . . . She was in trouble and had no money . . . Around that time,

---

174. LF, Transcript, 8.
175. LF, Transcript, 9.

> I received a large sum of money after sharing my testimony at a church. Suddenly, she came to mind. Before, I would never have considered helping her . . . But I thought, 'Let me help her!' This money is not mine but God's. That was the change I experienced.[176]

> I am not naturally patient . . . However, after my conversion, the greatest change in my life was a shift in my desires—I no longer wanted to keep asking God for things, but instead, I wanted to become someone the LORD could use . . . The only thing I ask of the LORD now is whether I have lived according to his will . . . My daily prayer is, 'Was I humble? Did I treat others with humility?' In the past, when conflicts arose, I would yell at people. But now, I apologize first. I tell them it is my fault. I have kept my focus on Jesus . . . I didn't realize how much my life was changing, but those around me told me that I had changed a lot.[177]

In this way, the transformation in the participants' lives was evident to those around them. While many were in the ongoing process of internalizing God's Word, there came a pivotal moment when they experienced God's full embrace through his Word, resulting in his presence being manifested in their lives. The stories shared above illustrate this transformation, demonstrating how their encounters with God reshaped their thoughts, actions, and relationships. These profound experiences became a powerful testimony to God's transformative work, revealing the deep changes that emerged from their growing relationship with him.

Stepping back to summarize the broader category of *Experiencing God*, it is evident that internalizing God's Word requires time and effort. Yet, through this process, participants also experienced the joy and love that came from encountering him. This internalization signified that God's Word had become an inseparable part of their being. Once God took hold of them through his Word, his kingdom was made manifest in their lives. They became vessels through whom the reality of God's kingdom was revealed to the world, impacting others and reflecting his character in their daily lives.

---

176. NM, Transcript, 8.
177. NM, Transcript, 7.

Comparative Analysis of the Main Categories and Themes

According to Strauss and Corbin, the method of constant comparison is both useful and essential in qualitative analysis, as it allows concepts within the data to be systematically compared with one another to identify differences, similarities, and underlying relationships.[178] By applying this approach, researchers can discern patterns and establish connections between key concepts. This section presents a comparative analysis of the major themes and categories identified in the previous sections. Through this process, the key factors influencing worldview transformation and their interrelationships will be examined.

The analysis includes multiple comparisons between themes and categories. First, four pairs of comparisons between two categories or themes are presented: (1) Life Prior to Conversion and Conversion Motives, (2) Life Prior to Conversion and Life After Conversion, (3) Receiving Enlightenment and Knowledge of God and Repentance for Renewal, and (4) Receiving Enlightenment and Knowledge of God and Facing Challenges and Longing for Transformation. Following these, one set of comparisons involves four interconnected themes: (5) Receiving Enlightenment and Knowledge of God, Repentance for Renewal, Facing Challenges and Longing for Transformation, and Experiencing God through the Word. Additionally, two sets of comparisons among three themes are included: (6) Receiving Enlightenment and Knowledge of God, Internalization, and Experiencing God through the Word, and (7) Receiving Enlightenment and Knowledge of God, Experiencing God through the Word, and Evidence of Transformation.

Comparing Life Prior to Conversion with Conversion Motives

The research showed that the themes identified in the category *Life Prior to Conversion contributed* to the development of *Conversion Motives*. The lives of the participants prior to their conversion varied. However, in general, they had no choice but to adhere to the regime's guidelines uniformly, at least until North Korea's distribution system collapsed. Unsurprisingly, almost half of the participants expressed absolute loyalty to the Supreme Leader (9/17). However, some participants described their lives as characterized by uncertainty (7/13), primarily due to the discrimination they

---

178. Strauss and Corbin, *Qualitative Research (1990)*, 60–80.

faced because of their disadvantaged family background. They also shared their struggles with numerous unanswered questions about life.

As the North Korean economy began to falter, the worldview of its people started to crumble, much like the collapse of a spine, regardless of their stance toward the regime. This led to significant challenges, such as trauma and crisis-induced struggles (15/77), as well as mental and emotional hardships (10/24). Under the regime, many individuals faced severe deficiencies in nearly every aspect of life, which fueled their aspirations for money, freedom, knowledge, success, and a noble life (9/18).

The motives behind conversion appear to be closely linked to an individual's circumstances before conversion. The participants' vulnerability—arising from a lack of safety, security, and provision—along with their disappointment in the Supreme Leader due to the failure of the trusted ideology (15/23), led them to look beyond their current circumstances with various longings and aspirations (10/24). These needs were largely met through encounters with the community of believers and missionaries in transit nations.

As if God had been waiting for them, the Holy Spirit came upon them, revealing who God is and what his will is for them. He made himself known through the sacrificial lives of the missionaries, sermons, Scripture reading and study and answered prayers. As a result, their confused and insecure lives found new direction and purpose, bringing comfort to many participants struggling with emotional and mental difficulties. Diagram 1 below compares life prior to conversion and conversion motives.

Diagram 1. Comparing Life Prior to Conversion with Conversion Motives

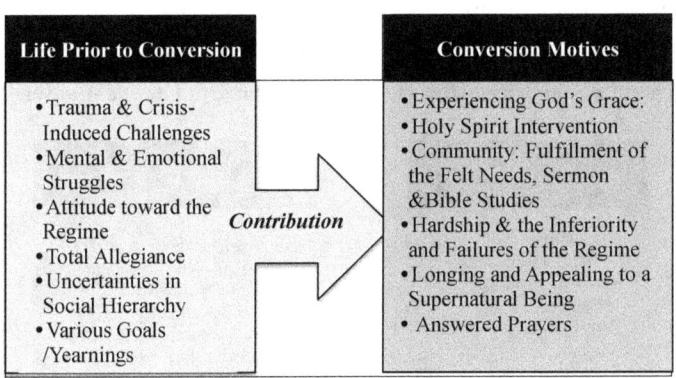

Comparing Life Prior to Conversion with Life after Conversion

The research showed that the themes identified in the category *Life Prior to Conversion continued* to *Life After Conversion*. During the process of transforming their worldview, the majority of participants encountered challenges stemming from their limited understanding of God, self, and the kingdom. Additionally, in submitting to God's lordship, the participants discovered numerous idols in their lives, along with mental, moral, and interpersonal struggles.

Notably, more than half of the participants identified anger, bitterness, and unforgiveness as struggles, and the research found that these issues were also related to their relational difficulties. Specifically, thirteen out of fifteen participants (87 percent) who had experienced trauma and mental and emotional struggles in *Life Prior to Conversion* still struggled with the same issues despite having been Christians for an average of 14 years. Eleven participants identified various lasting effects of the North Korean system as challenges, particularly in the areas of self-accomplishment and humanism rooted in Juche ideology.

The research found that eight out of eleven participants (73 percent) who retained residual influences from the North Korean system in *Life After Conversion* were the ones who had been absolutely loyal to the Supreme Leader in *Life Prior to Conversion*. Thus, it can be assumed that those who had lived a life of absolute loyalty are still under significant influence from its lasting effects, even in *Life After Conversion*. Additionally, five out of nine participants who had previously pursued various goals such as money, freedom, knowledge, and success identified various forms of idolization as an ongoing struggle (56 percent) in *Life After Conversion*. Diagram 2 below presents the comparison between the two categories.

Diagram 2. Comparing Life Prior to Conversion with Life after Conversion

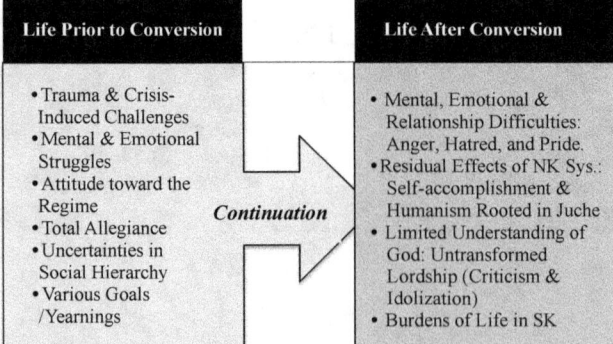

Findings

Comparing Receiving Enlightenment and Knowledge of God with Repentance for Renewal

Research indicated that the theme Receiving Enlightenment and Knowledge of God brought *conviction*, leading to the theme Repentance for Renewal. God's intervening presence in the lives of the participants took diverse ways. They received spiritual enlightenment and knowledge of God, specifically through revelatory insights, corrections, and guidance. God, through his Word, convicted them in areas such as idol worship, self-righteousness, immorality, and critical judgment of others. In their studying and meditation of Scripture, some participants gained a deeper knowledge of God, particularly insights into his nature. In addition, the participants gained an understanding of how to overcome difficulties and grow in their love for the LORD.

Notably, when God convicted them of their sins, they were led to repentance in areas such as unresolved lordship to God, immorality, self-accomplishment, anger, and bitterness.

As God purified them through repentance, some participants, including EF and QF, received further enlightenment and knowledge of God and his will. After repenting of her past sin of stealing, Participant EF heard God's voice saying, "The old is gone, and the new has come." Moreover, that night, God revealed the kingdom of God to her in a dream, igniting a deep desire to share the gospel. Similarly, after Participant QF repented of her indifference toward other suffering defectors, God took her in spirit to North Korea, showing her a future of freedom without concentration camps or prisons. After this experience, she was healed of the chronic coldness in her hands and feet.

These cases demonstrate that God led the participants to repentance, and after they repented, he removed the obstacles in their lives and drew them into a closer relationship with him. The analysis indicates that the themes of Receiving Enlightenment and Knowledge of God and Repentance are inseparably connected and follow a sequential order. In other words, in the process of experiencing God, particularly when he granted them spiritual enlightenment and knowledge of himself, they became *convicted* of their sins and repented. Diagram 3 below illustrates the relationship between these themes.

Diagram 3. Comparing Receiving Enlightenment with Repentance for Renewal

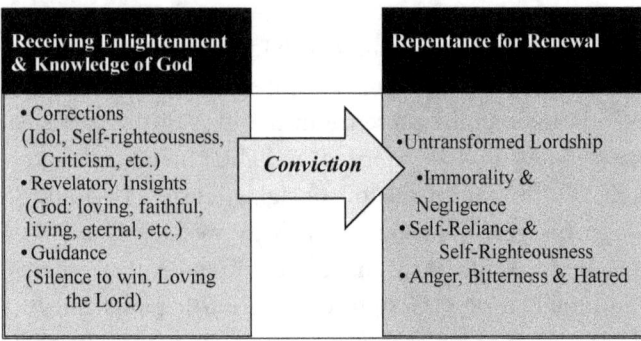

Comparing Receiving Enlightenment and Knowledge of God with Facing Challenges and Longing for Transformation

The research found that the relationship between the two themes Receiving Enlightenment and Knowledge of God and Facing Challenges and Longing for Transformation, can be understood as a process of spiritual *awakening*. God intervened in the participants' lives by imparting enlightenment and knowledge of him through revelatory insights, corrections, and guidance. As a result, his Word challenged some participants, creating inner struggles for sanctification. More than half of the participants started longing to pursue a holy life, trust in God rather than their own understanding, and grow in Christlikeness. Half of the participants desired to see God's kingdom realized in North Korea, while others longed to understand his plan and perspectives for their lives. Nine participants expressed a longing for a deeper relationship with God.

In comparing these two themes, it becomes clear that the first theme *awakened* in them a longing for transformation and presented challenges, which ultimately drew them closer to God, deepening their relationship with Him. Diagram 4 illustrates the relationship between these themes.

Findings

Diagram 4. Comparing Receiving Enlightenment and Knowledge of God with Facing Challenges and Longing for Transformation

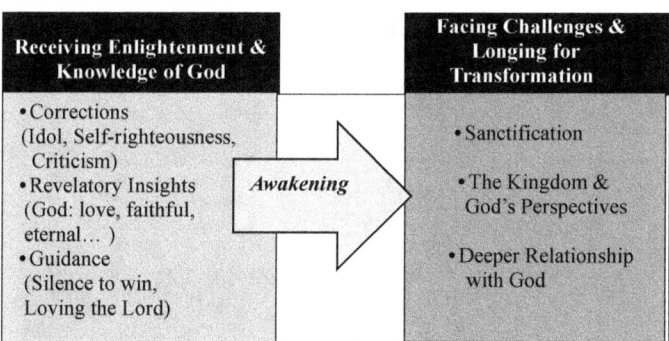

Comparing Receiving Enlightenment and Knowledge, Repentance, Facing Challenges and Longing for Transformation, and Experiencing God through the Word

The previous two comparisons have noted the relationships among the three themes: Receiving Enlightenment and Knowledge of God, Repentance for Spiritual Renewal, and Facing Challenges and Longing for Transformation. This section extends the discussion by examining another theme, Experiencing God through the Word, in relation to Receiving Enlightenment and Knowledge of God. For participants AF, GF, KF, RF, QF, LF, TM, DM, and HM, the moment they received enlightenment and knowledge of God, they simultaneously encountered God personally. When TM heard God's voice affirming his love—free from coercion or anger, contrary to his previous beliefs—he encountered the very essence of God's Word. This activation of divine love healed his past wounds, transformed his life, and empowered him to extend that same love to others Thus, in comparing these two themes Receiving Enlightenment and Knowledge of God and Experiencing God through His Word, it becomes evident that the former acts as an *activation*, leading to a direct experience of God. Diagram 5 below presents the comparisons among the four themes.

Diagram 5. Comparing Receiving Enlightenment, Repentance for Renewal, Facing Challenges, and Experiencing God through His Word

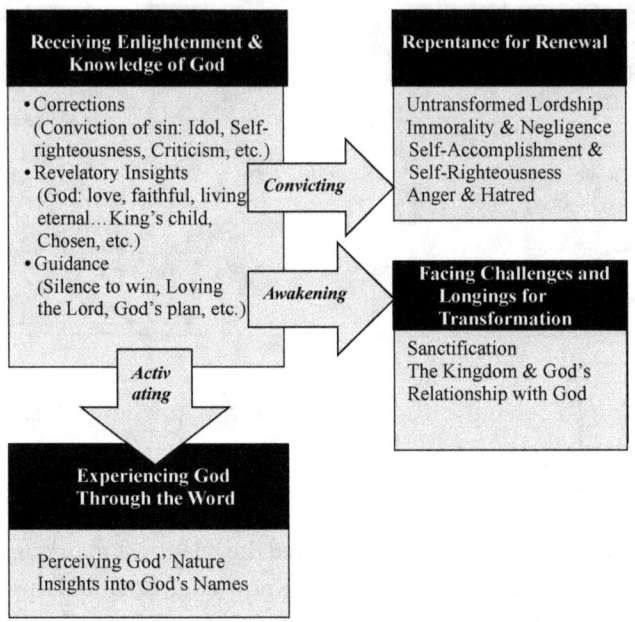

Comparing Receiving Enlightenment and Knowledge of God, Internalization, and Experiencing God through the Word

When God intervened in the participants' lives by imparting divine enlightenment and a deeper knowledge of him—whether through revelatory insights, corrections, or guidance—some responded with repentance, while others perceived it as a challenge or developed a longing for transformation. Additionally, while some participants immediately embraced the Word as their own, others entered a process of internalization. For example, Participant LF was challenged to love her enemies. In response, she began seeking to understand God's perspective, desiring to align her heart with his. This search led her to experience the love of God, who also loved her enemies, ultimately bringing her to her knees in prayer as she was shaped into Christlikeness in this area. Observing her process, she first received enlightenment—the call to love her enemies—then sought to understand God's heart (knowledge of God) on the matter until she gained a deeper understanding of his perspective and experienced his love (experiencing

Findings

God through the Word). Through the internalization process, she continued to hold onto this enlightenment, praying for transformation so that she could truly reflect Christ (Christ-likeness) in her actions.

The relationship between Receiving Enlightenment and Knowledge of God and Internalization of God's Word can be understood as the process of *assimilating* God's truth into one's life, while the relationship between Internalization of God's Word and Experiencing God through the Word involves *deepening* one's relationship with God through the transformative encounter with that truth. As the participants experienced God through the Word more deeply through the process of internalization, they repeated the cycle of receiving further enlightenment and knowledge of God. Diagram 6 below presents the comparisons among these three themes.

Diagram 6. Comparing Receiving Enlightenment, Internalization, and Experiencing God through the Word

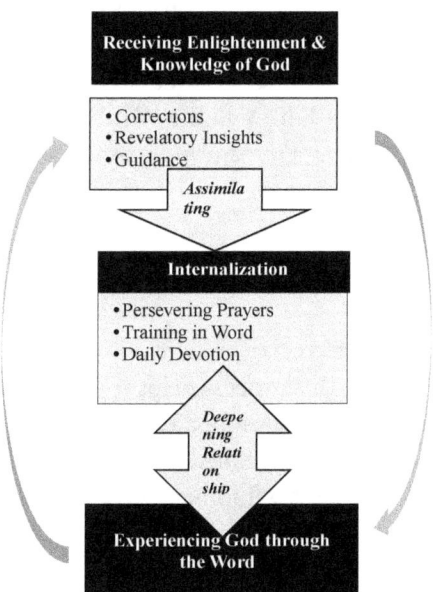

Comparing Enlightenment and Knowledge, Experiencing God through the Word, and Evidence of Transformation

Observing the relationship between Receiving Enlightenment and Knowledge of God and Experiencing God through the Word leads to the conclusion that God *activated* the participants' encounter with his Word, enabling them to experience him personally. Alongside these two themes, a third theme will be added to the matrix—Evidence of Transformation. The participants—AF, GF, KF, RF, QF, LF, TM, DM, HM, NM, OM, and SF—experienced God as soon as they received enlightenment and knowledge of him. However, seven of these 12 participants progressed further into the theme of Evidence of Transformation, demonstrating visible changes in their lives through the Word they received. In other words, their encounter with the Word not only allowed them to experience God but also transformed their lives in ways that those around them could clearly perceive. For instance, Participant DM, a former political officer in North Korea, fully embraced God as the true Way rather than communism upon receiving enlightenment of God and experiencing him. This experience became firmly established in him, reshaping his worldview in alignment with the system of God's kingdom. His heart was firmly convinced of God's absoluteness, and since then, in various aspects of his life—such as culture and entertainment—he has refused to watch any movie or drama unless it aligns with the order of God's kingdom. The relationship between the theme Experiencing God through the Word and Evidence of Transformation can be understood as a *transforming* process. Diagram 7 presents a comparison of these three themes.

Theoretical Coding

Theoretical coding, also referred to as *selective coding*, involves integrating and refining categories.[179] This process helps specify the potential relationships between the categories developed during focused coding.[180] At this stage, the major categories are unified into a comprehensive theoretical framework, shaping the research findings into a coherent theory.[181]

---

179. Corbin and Strauss, *Qualitative Research 2e*, 143.
180. Charmaz, *Grounded Theory*, 63.
181. Corbin and Strauss, *Qualitative research 2e*, 143.

Diagram 7. Comparing Receiving Enlightenment, Experiencing God through the Word, and Evidence of Transformation

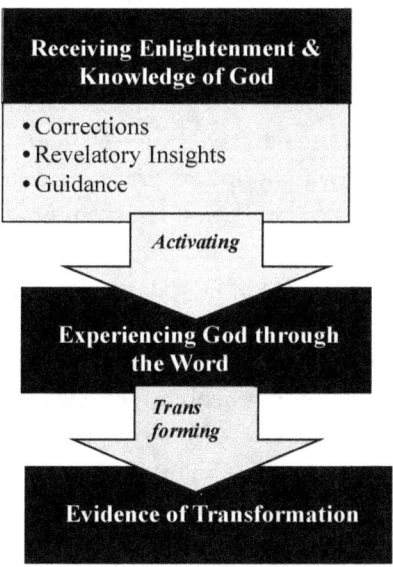

Theoretical Integration of the Analysis of Worldview Transformation

The purpose of *theoretical integration* is to construct a theory.[182] The concepts developed during initial and focused coding must be connected and elaborated upon to form a coherent theoretical framework. In this process, the key factors, themes, and categories influencing worldview transformation, along with the core category or theme, are identified. Figure 1 below presents these key factors, themes, and categories in relation to the process of worldview transformation.

The first step in constructing a theory was identifying the key factors, as shown in Figure 1. To briefly explain their relationships, the key factor *Life Prior to Conversion contributed* to the formation of the *Motives of Conversion*. Many participants' spiritual and physical needs were met through interactions with the community of believers and missionaries in transit nations. The sacrificial lives of missionaries, Bible studies, and answered prayers played a crucial role in leading them to an encounter with God and

182. Corbin and Strauss, *Qualitative Research 3e,* 103.

a conversion experience. However, in the process of worldview transformation, participants faced challenges. As the key factor *Life after Conversion* illustrates, many struggled due to a limited understanding of God, unresolved anger, bitterness, and unforgiveness—issues that were a *continuation* of the difficulties they faced prior to conversion, which also contributed to relational struggles. Over time, the theme God's Intervention worked in their lives, *leading* to the theme Receiving Enlightenment and Knowledge of God as they engaged with Scripture, prayer, and the Holy Spirit's guidance. Through this process, God *convicted* them of areas misaligned with his kingdom, prompting Repentance for Renewal. Additionally, Receiving Enlightenment and Knowledge of God *awakened* them, challenging them and instilling a longing for transformation, drawing them closer to him. A key component of the transformation was Internalization of God's Word, which played a crucial role in enabling participants to Experience God through the Word. This process of internalization was accompanied by persistent prayer and meditation. As a result, participants' relationship with God *deepened*, leading to further enlightenment and knowledge of him. As their relationship with God deepened, they became more closely aligned with his Word—a transformation that can be described as a shift toward a biblical worldview. Diagram 8 below illustrates the worldview transformation process of the 20 participants, detailing the interconnections among key factors. A brief explanation of their relationships follows the diagram. Additionally, Figure 2 presents the dynamics of God's Word in transformation toward a biblical worldview.

FINDINGS

Figure 1. Factors Influencing Worldview Transformation and Its Process: Insights from Themes and Categories Grounded in the Collected Data

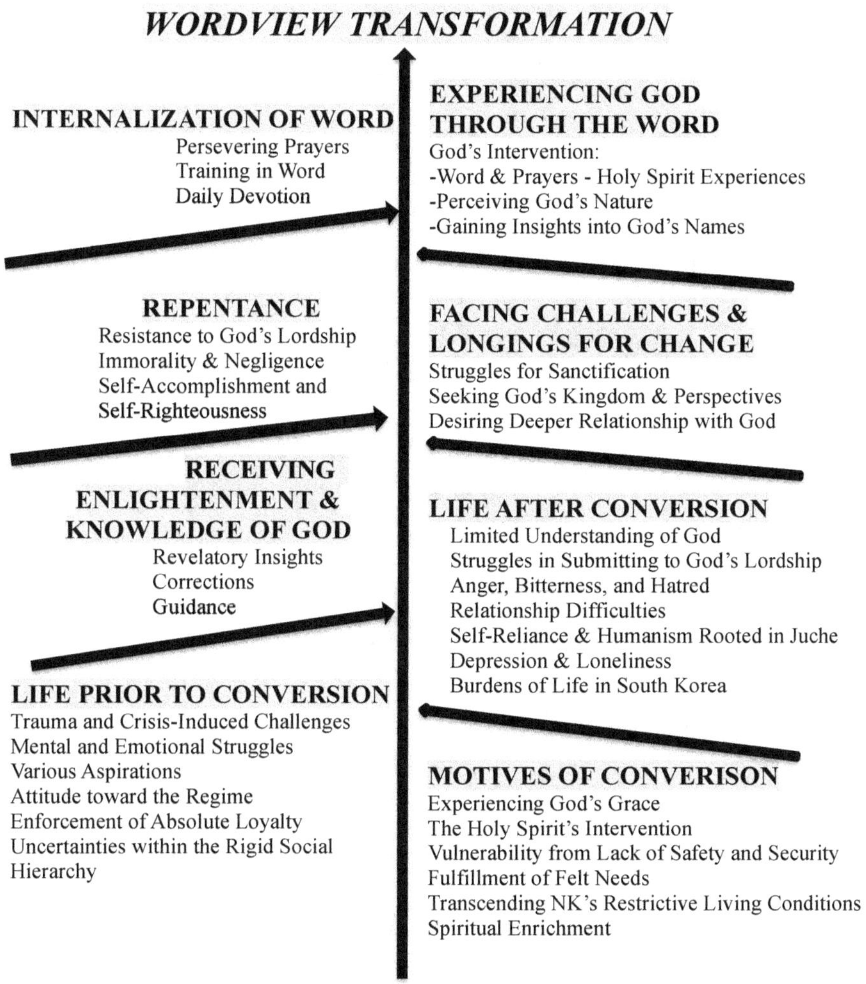

WORDVIEW TRANSFORMATION

INTERNALIZATION OF WORD
Persevering Prayers
Training in Word
Daily Devotion

EXPERIENCING GOD THROUGH THE WORD
God's Intervention:
-Word & Prayers - Holy Spirit Experiences
-Perceiving God's Nature
-Gaining Insights into God's Names

REPENTANCE
Resistance to God's Lordship
Immorality & Negligence
Self-Accomplishment and
Self-Righteousness

FACING CHALLENGES & LONGINGS FOR CHANGE
Struggles for Sanctification
Seeking God's Kingdom & Perspectives
Desiring Deeper Relationship with God

RECEIVING ENLIGHTENMENT & KNOWLEDGE OF GOD
Revelatory Insights
Corrections
Guidance

LIFE AFTER CONVERSION
Limited Understanding of God
Struggles in Submitting to God's Lordship
Anger, Bitterness, and Hatred
Relationship Difficulties
Self-Reliance & Humanism Rooted in Juche
Depression & Loneliness
Burdens of Life in South Korea

LIFE PRIOR TO CONVERSION
Trauma and Crisis-Induced Challenges
Mental and Emotional Struggles
Various Aspirations
Attitude toward the Regime
Enforcement of Absolute Loyalty
Uncertainties within the Rigid Social Hierarchy

MOTIVES OF CONVERISON
Experiencing God's Grace
The Holy Spirit's Intervention
Vulnerability from Lack of Safety and Security
Fulfillment of Felt Needs
Transcending NK's Restrictive Living Conditions
Spiritual Enrichment

Diagram 8. The Process of Worldview Transformation & Correlation among the Key Factors

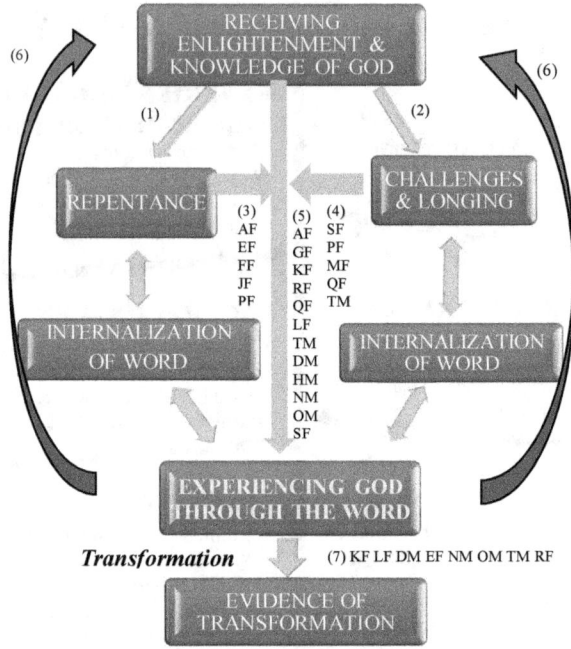

1. All participants (except GF) received conviction from the enlightenment and knowledge of God through God's intervention, and they were led to repentance for renewal.

2. All participants, except JF and LF, faced challenges and/or developed a longing for transformation as a result of receiving enlightenment and knowledge of God through his intervention.

3. Some participants experienced a single moment of repentance, followed by encountering/experiencing God through his Word (e.g., repenting trusting in their wisdom, relational conflict, etc.).

4. Others faced significant challenges and, in response, experienced God's presence by obeying his Word.

5. Some participants immediately experienced God through his Word after receiving enlightenment and knowledge of God.

6. Participants on the left arrow were in the process of internalizing God's Word through repentance, while those on the right arrow did so through developing longing or facing challenges in their pursuit of God. This process involved persevering in prayer and immersing themselves in the Word. Participants on the left arrow grappled with issues such as CF (criticism), DM (hatred and ego), EF (anger), FF (violence and idol worship), HM (self-accomplishment), IM (self-accomplishment), JF (anger), SF (self-accomplishment), and TM (self-accomplishment). On the right arrow, participants were associated with AF (Immanuel), BF (answered prayers), CF (longing for holiness), DM (longing to be like Christ), EF (honesty/purity challenges), GF (unity in the body of Christ), KF (being critical), LF (loving enemies), MF (financial challenges), NM (Christlikeness), OM (forgiving the unlovable), PF (awareness and presence of God), QF (training in the Word), and RF (knowing and seeking God's will). As participants progressed, they experienced a deepening relationship with God and gained a greater understanding of him and his will. The side arrows illustrate the flow from experiencing God through the Word to acquiring more enlightenment and knowledge of God. Some participants then repeated the cycle of repentance, facing challenges, or longing for transformation, while others immediately experienced God more deeply, building upon their new understanding of him

7. These participants demonstrated evidence of transformation toward a biblical worldview through repeatedly experiencing God through the Word. They shared that these transformations were visible to those around them, including their spouses, co-workers, and members of the organizations they were a part of.

The following words were being internalized and taking root within them:

RF: She was deeply impacted by the truth that *God is eternal, and Jesus Christ was resurrected.* These words gave her the will to live and renewed her hope. Moreover, the image of her loving and kind earthly father helped her embrace God as her own loving Father in a profound way. Her transformation became even more evident, as she had once been devastated by Kim Il Sung's death, having placed all her hope and trust in him.

TM: After experiencing *Almighty God*—who miraculously caused his hair to grow on skin without pores and rescued him at the North Korean border while smuggling Bibles—TM was completely taken hold of by God. This encounter made him fearless in sharing the gospel inside North Korea.

KF: She internalized the truth that *Jesus Christ died for my sin*. Through this process, God removed the anger within her, leading her to experience His love and care. He confirmed this transformation by giving her Deut 28:8: "The LORD will grant that the enemies who rise against you will be defeated before you. They will come at you from one direction but flee from you in seven."

LF: *Loving the enemies*: "How much did he love me that he died for me?" I thought. "When his love enters my heart at such depth, loving enemies can no longer be impossible." And, she said, "When God's Word and the Spirit work together, his Word takes root in me, and I no longer waver."

DM: God's Word immediately took root in DM's heart: *Jesus is the Way, the Truth, and the Life—Neither communism nor capitalism. Jesus, the absolute truth*! He embraced Jesus as the absolute truth, marking a fundamental shift in his worldview. This new understanding opened the way for him to fully embrace God's kingdom.

EF: God removed her past sins, confirming this through the Word: "The old is gone, the new has come." She came to understand God as *a God of miracles, a God who answers her prayers, and a God who is always with her, listening*. In communion with God, she lived a lifestyle of worship, spending time in her prayer closet. She used to go before God, acknowledging her tendency toward self-accomplishment, influenced by the NK system. However, her victory over this was clearly demonstrated in the story she shared of how she learned to be led by God.

NM: He immediately experienced the rooting of God's great love through a vision of *God's love shown on the cross*. The healing of his sorrows over the innocent children who had passed away, which had caused him to distance himself from God, became possible when he understood that it is God's dominion, not his own.

FINDINGS

OM: After 8 years of imprisonment, the only realization OM came to was that he should live only *for God* and *according to his will*, not relying on the righteousness that had sustained him during his time in prison. This marked a significant shift in his perspective and opens a new way for him to embrace God's kingdom.

Figure 2. The Dynamics of God's Word in the Transformation Process

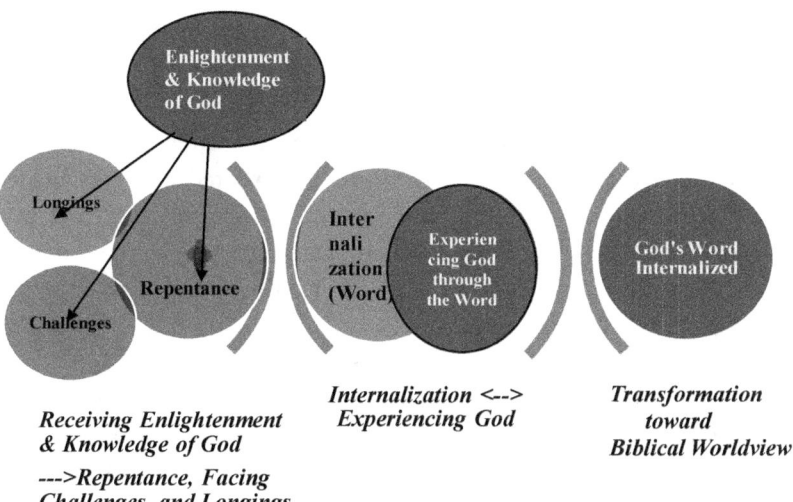

Receiving Enlightenment & Knowledge of God ---> *Repentance, Facing Challenges, and Longings*   *Internalization <--> Experiencing God*   *Transformation toward Biblical Worldview*

The researcher presents Figure 2 above to illustrate the dynamics of God's Word in the transformation process. For example, Participant LF received God's Word about loving her enemies with the same love Christ demonstrated on the cross. She longed to embody this love so that she could extend it to others as Christ does. As she internalized the Word through deep meditation and persevering prayer, she intermittently experienced God's love. Her meditation deepened as she focused on the cross of Jesus Christ, and she sought to understand God's perspective on her enemies. This led her to a profound realization: Christ Jesus loves them just as much as He loves her. In God's perfect timing, she understood that the Word itself had united her with him in this matter, and she experienced a deep sense of oneness with God. As a result, she was able to forgive those who had reviled against her and received them in her heart with love, providing clear evidence of her transformation.

Story Line of Worldview Transformation of 20 North Korean Defectors

The technique of writing a storyline helps integrate key concepts and facilitates the identification of the core category. Concepts are connected through statements that define their relationships, weaving them into a cohesive narrative. The key themes include the participants' context, the factors influencing worldview transformation, the transformation process itself, and the relationships among these elements. After presenting the storyline of the 20 participants' worldview transformation, a paradigm model summarizing the process and key factors will be introduced in Figure 3.

The 20 participants are all North Korean defectors currently living in South Korea. Before their conversion, they shared a common background—life under a system of communism or collectivism. The data reveals that some participants were deeply committed to serving the will of their Supreme Leader, fully indoctrinated into the ideology of the regime. Others, particularly those from lower social strata, lived in insecurity and confusion, denigrated and shamed by the regime.

Existential questions beyond Juche ideology remained unanswered, as the system provided no framework for contemplating personal worth, aspirations, or life's purpose. Without a philosophical foundation outside of Juche, participants struggled to make sense of life and death. Some, driven by the harsh realities of their circumstances, pursued wealth as a means of survival, while others sought freedom, a dignified life, knowledge, or even a way to challenge and change the North Korean regime.

As the North Korean economy, including the rationing system, began to collapse in the mid-1990s, the worldview of the North Korean people started to unravel. The regime's failure led to widespread disillusionment, resentment, and deep dissatisfaction. As they faced severe crises, many experienced hopelessness and powerlessness, enduring starvation, human trafficking, and the hardships of defection at great personal risk. Alongside these struggles, they encountered an identity crisis and a profound disorientation regarding life's meaning and worth as their existence became consumed by the desperate fight for survival. Naturally, mental and emotional distress followed, with many suffering from depression, insecurity, and anxiety. These conditions contributed to their motives for conversion to the Christian faith. Their vulnerability—resulting from a lack of safety, security, and provision—was significantly alleviated by believers in the transit nations, who cared for both their physical and spiritual needs.

Findings

For some, the God they had desperately sought in their suffering was revealed to be the God of the Bible. Other major factors that opened their hearts to Jesus Christ included *experiencing God's gracious nature*—such as the sacrificial love of Christ—through the presence of the Holy Spirit and the lives of missionaries who embodied the character and work of Jesus. Additional influences included listening to sermons, experiencing love, watching Christian films, encountering God's Word in their personal lives, witnessing answered prayers, and the impact of Christian family members in North Korea. As they encountered God and his gracious nature, they also began to grasp his will and calling for their lives and the kingdom of God, primarily through the Holy Spirit's work and reading the Word of God. For the participants, this marked the very first stage of experiencing and encountering God.

Through conversion, their chaotic and insecure lives found new direction and purpose. Many participants who had struggled with emotional and mental distress were comforted and healed as they encountered new emotions in God—peace, security, joy, hope, and a newfound sense of brightness. A major transformation in their lives resulted from *experiencing God*, which profoundly shaped their self-identity and self-perception. They came to know God as Love, Provider, Father, Creator, Master—eternal, living, and actively at work, even in North Korea. Their newfound identity as children of God transformed how they saw themselves: they were now worthy, precious, loved, and chosen to serve North Korea. Consequently, their outlook on life and its purpose shifted toward a God-centered perspective. They longed to know God more, set new priorities, and reinterpreted their past hardships in light of his work in their lives. Additionally, their attitude toward others changed, and they became more generous and valued the fellowship of believers.

After their conversion, participants faced significant challenges due to their limited understanding of God, self, and the kingdom of God. The greatest difficulty stemmed from an untransformed sense of lordship. Many wrestled with issues such as criticism, unforgiveness, and the idolization of North Korea, ministry, self, children, and money. Some also struggled with unbiblical views of God, perceiving him as angry, indifferent, or unfaithful. For these participants, it was difficult to comprehend a loving God who had allowed so many innocent lives to perish from starvation in North Korea or who had permitted the injustices they endured in transit nations. In one case, this struggle led a participant to turn away from God for 8 years.

In the areas of mental, moral, and relational difficulties, participants commonly identified anger, hatred, depression, and interpersonal conflicts as major struggles. While these challenges were partially shaped by their experiences in North Korea and China, they were also deeply rooted in the residual influence of the North Korean system and the humanistic ideology of Juche. Some participants recognized their tendency toward self-accomplishment and saw it as something to overcome, while others were unaware of this inclination, as it was so deeply ingrained in them. Blind obedience—rooted in North Korea's culture of idolization and its utopian dream, which was not the kingdom of God that Jesus preached—was another major struggle participants identified.

When faced with these difficulties, God intervened in their lives in various ways. He granted them enlightenment and a deeper knowledge of himself through spiritual disciplines such as prayer, reading Scripture, meditating on the Word, and fasting. While many participants mentioned God's intervention in their transformation, such as hearing his voice, seeing visions, receiving impressions, and experiencing physical healing, the primary focus was on their deepening experience of God himself. The enlightenment and knowledge of him that they received had a corrective nature, along with revelatory insights and guidance. When God revealed himself as loving, forgiving, holy, eternal, living, and patient—answering their prayers and calling them to work for his kingdom—they were moved not only intellectually but also emotionally. Some responded with gratitude, joy, and hope, while others were overwhelmed with tears of comfort.

Additionally, God granted them a clearer understanding of his will, guiding them in how to navigate relationships, establish priorities, and cultivate a life of prayer. In response to these divine interventions, participants experienced challenges and deep longings in areas of sanctification, the kingdom of God, and their relationship with him. Some participants were challenged to love the unlovable, change their critical attitudes toward others, step out of their comfort zones, and break free from unbiblical thinking. At the same time, many experienced an intense longing to become more like Jesus Christ—embodying his love, pursuing a closer relationship with him, and submitting to his lordship in trust. Others sought clarity on God's will for their lives and were deeply committed to evangelism.

At the same time, out of his love for them, God convicted participants of their sins—idolization, controlling tendencies, failure to prioritize his kingdom, criticism, self-righteousness, unforgiveness, anger, distorted perspectives of God, relational struggles, and reliance on self-accomplishment. These issues were recognized as obstacles to the advancement of God's kingdom within them and also hindered their transformation. Additionally, upon receiving enlightenment and knowledge of God, some participants experienced his Word as *rhema,* and in that moment, they *encountered the living Word, Jesus Himself,* deeply in their hearts.

Participants repeatedly went through a series of processes—receiving God's Word, being challenged and filled with longing, experiencing repentance, and directly encountering God through the *rhema* word. Through these repeated experiences, the Word was *internalized* in their hearts, a process that required perseverance in prayer and meditation on his Word. During this phase, God's Word restructured their thought systems and broke down strongholds, including criticism, hatred, anger, self-accomplishment, and self-righteousness—many of which stemmed from Juche ideology. At the same time, God drew closer to those whose hearts burned with longing for him. Through these repeated *experiences of God through the Word*, he granted fresh insights into his nature, continually drawing them back to the theme of receiving further enlightenment and knowledge of him (See Diagram 8).

As participants went through this transformative cycle, God, in his perfect timing, completed the process of aligning their lives with the Scripture he had given them—leading to a transformation toward a biblical worldview. The Bible captures this process in Eph 3:17–19: "So that Christ may dwell in your hearts through faith. And I pray that you, being rooted and established in love, may have power, together with all the saints, to grasp how wide and long and high and deep is the love of Christ." Each transformation represented a deeper rooting of God's Word in their hearts, a work that God himself established in love. Some participants testified that even the smallest transformations in their lives were evident to those around them, allowing God's glory to shine through them for his honor.

In conclusion, worldview transformation belongs to God's dominion because he is the very Word and the One who brings it to completion (Isa 55:10–11). For participants who lived under the North Korean regime, witnessed its economic downfall, defected to transit nations, and eventually arrived in South Korea, God has been shifting them from the system of Kim's kingdom to the system of his kingdom. He is actively at work among them, and as Phil 1:6 affirms, "He who began a good work in you will carry it on to completion until the day of Christ Jesus." This transformative work in their lives took place through experiencing God. The theme of *Experiencing God* included several dimensions: the Internalization of God's Word, Experiencing God through the Word, Divinely Bestowed Emotion, and Evidence of Transformation. While all these aspects played significant roles in the participants' worldview transformation, the very heart of this transformation was rooted in *experiencing God through his Word*.

Experiencing God through the Word, rather than simply acquiring enlightenment and knowledge, was the key to their worldview transformation. In this process, they not only tasted God's goodness but also experienced divinely bestowed emotions such as love, joy, freedom, confidence, and fearlessness—each contributing to profound heart transformation, as described in Eph 3:17–19. While they received enlightenment, faced challenges, and repented for spiritual renewal, true transformation unfolded as they internalized God's Word and encountered him on a deeper level. This intimate experience of God was crucial in strengthening their relationship with him, allowing them to experience his love in more profound and meaningful ways. Moreover, this process reshaped their hearts, thoughts, and actions, aligning them with God's kingdom. Their transformation was not merely intellectual but relational, resulting in visible evidence of change in their lives. Figure 3 summarizes this transformative process as reflected in the participants' testimonies.

Summary of Theoretical Coding

A major category that encompasses all others is *Experiencing God*. The participants first encountered God at the time of their conversion, primarily through direct experiences of God and the Holy Spirit. However, their transformation deepened over time as they experienced God's continued intervention—through enlightenment and knowledge of him and his will. God convicted them in areas of their lives that were not aligned with his kingdom, challenging them and stirring within them a longing to draw closer to him.

The process of internalizing the Word required perseverance in prayer and meditation on Scripture. Each time participants engaged in this process, God revealed himself anew, leading to fresh experiences of his presence and further enlightenment and knowledge of him. As they went through this cycle repeatedly, God, in his perfect timing, completed his work of shaping them through his Word. In the areas of life surrendered

FINDINGS

to him, God's kingship was established, marking a transformation toward a biblical worldview. This transformation is an ongoing process, continuing until the day of Christ Jesus. However, while on earth, believers are called to reflect God's glory in the world. The church, therefore, must rise to the fullness of Christ, allowing God's Word to take root step by step as he speaks daily into their lives.

Figure 3. Paradigm Model according to Worldview Transformation Phenomenon

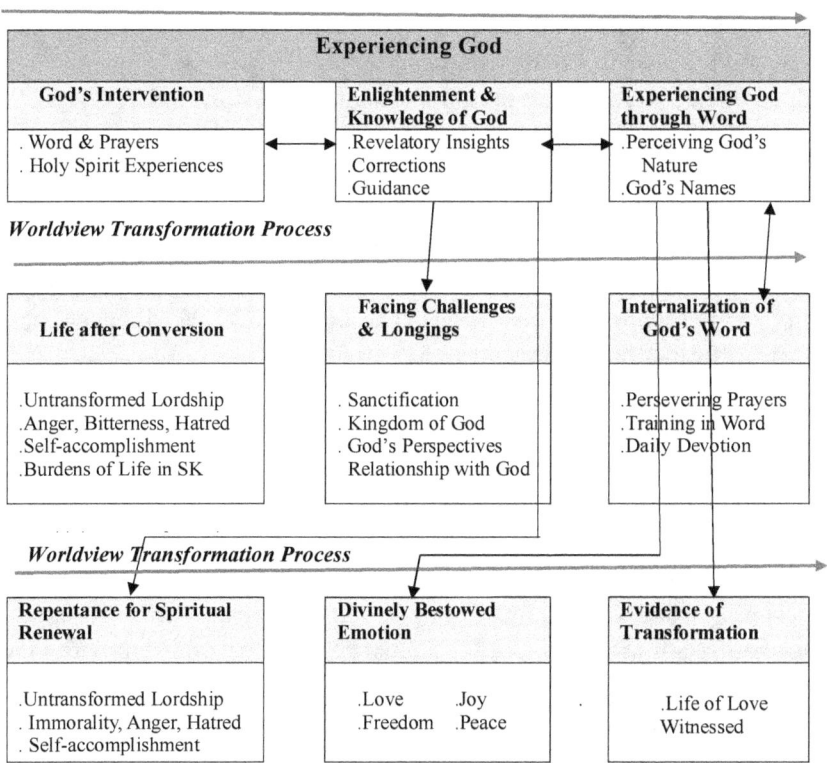

Given that *Experiencing God* is the overarching concept, *Experiencing God through the Word* becomes a more specific and central theme for worldview transformation. It represents the process through which participants encounter God's transformative work in their lives, making it a crucial aspect of the broader concept of *Experiencing God*. This theme not only connects to the larger concept but also highlights the vital means by which participants engage with God. It is through this process—engaging with Scripture, alongside prayer and meditation—that their worldview is reshaped, and their spiritual renewal takes place. As a result, Experiencing God through the Word serves as a powerful focal point for the purpose of this research. Through this ongoing interaction with God's Word, God's presence becomes more real, leading to deeper understanding, inner transformation, and the establishment of his kingdom in their lives.

Regarding the impact of North Korean anti-Christian education, Juche ideology, and cultural influences, these factors had little immediate effect on participants at the time of their conversion. Their felt needs were met by the Christian community in transit nations, where they found new hope and purpose in Christ. This experience filled their spiritual void and helped them overcome past disappointment, depression, and hopelessness. However, as their faith and knowledge of Christ grew, the residual effects of the North Korean system and humanistic ideas rooted in Juche became evident. These influences surfaced as obstacles to their worldview transformation. Those unable to overcome these challenges risked becoming nominal or syncretic Christians. However, many participants, strengthened by the empowerment and love they received through God's Word, experienced true transformation.

In summary, although the overarching category that encompasses all others is *Experiencing God*, *Experiencing God through the Word* stands as the central theme that connects and integrates all other categories, capturing the essence of the research. The data revealed that as participants received God's enlightenment and knowledge of him, they opened their hearts to repentance, accepted challenges, and longed for more of him. Just as genuine trust between individuals develops over time through experience and relationship, so too did the participants' relationship with God. As participants engaged in the process of internalizing the Word, God continually revealed his love and deepened their relationship with him. During this time, God also worked to remove hindrances in their hearts, as illustrated in Diagram 8, and stirred deeper longings for him, drawing them into greater intimacy until they became united with his Word. In this way, God's lordship was firmly established, and his Word became deeply rooted in their lives, making their transformation visible to those around them. This constitutes a genuine transformation toward a biblical worldview.

Findings

Theory from the Research

The worldview of individuals formerly shaped by Juche ideology undergoes a profound transformation as they cultivate a deepening relationship with God, ultimately leading to unity with his Word. This transformation unfolds through the internalization of Scripture, sustained by persevering prayer. As participants progress in this journey, they experience God more intimately, gaining a deeper understanding of his character and purposes. The process continues until their lives are fully aligned with God's Word. Once Scripture takes root in this way, God's sovereignty and reign in the relevant areas of their lives become visible, often witnessed by those around them. This marks a significant shift toward a biblical worldview.

5

Conclusion

THE OBJECTIVE OF THIS research was to examine the factors and process underlying the transformation of North Korean defector Christians' worldviews into a biblical framework and to formulate a theory based on these findings using the Grounded Theory research methodology. As the concluding chapter, this section provides an overview of the research process, previously examined in detail, and presents a theory on the transformation of North Korean defector Christians' worldviews. This is followed by a discussion of prior studies on North Korean defectors, particularly those relevant to this research. The chapter concludes with an analysis of missiological implications for practice and recommendations for further research.

Summary of the Research Process

The data collection and analysis phases of this research can be summarized as follows. Given the limited research on the worldview transformation of North Korean defectors, the Grounded Theory methodology was deemed the most suitable approach for analyzing both the factors and the process underlying this phenomenon. Before conducting formal interviews, the researcher sought preliminary insights by consulting two defector ministers and securing their agreement to participate in pilot interviews. These initial interviews revealed that participants tended to focus excessively on certain topics that were not necessarily relevant to their worldview transformation. Recognizing this tendency, the researcher determined that some degree of guidance was necessary to keep the discussions focused. The recurring themes in these interviews centered on their conversion experiences and their present struggles. Consequently, the researcher concluded that a minimal interview framework was essential to ensure efficient use of time and to systematically gather data on both the factors and the process of their worldview transformation, allowing for a more comprehensive understanding of the subject.

Being mindful of these themes, the researcher conducted interviews with 20 North Korean defectors residing across South Korea, from Seoul to Jeju Island. Using open-ended questions, the interviews focused on significant moments of worldview transformation, spanning from their lives before conversion to the present, with the goal of developing a theory on this transformation. A few participants were already acquainted with the researcher and were deemed suitable for the study's objectives. The remaining participants were introduced by pastors, a school principal, and other participants who understood the purpose of the research and knew individuals who fit the study's criteria. As previously noted, theoretical sampling was employed to refine the emerging concepts and themes during data collection.

Second, the data collected from the 20 participants was transcribed in Korean to preserve its original meaning, resulting in a transcript exceeding 220 pages. To clarify underlying meanings or obtain more precise information, follow-up phone calls were conducted with five participants. The additional data collected was transcribed and incorporated into the respective participant's interview file, with the date of each follow-up recorded. Portions of the transcripts were translated into English by the researcher for inclusion in the research paper. Additionally, through informal discussions over meals with those who introduced the participants, as well as by attending Sunday worship services at their churches, the researcher gathered further insights related to the participants' worldview transformation. These interactions contributed to a clearer understanding of the data.

Third, the collected data was analyzed using NVivo 12 software to develop concepts, themes, and categories through constant comparison, from the open coding stage to selective coding. This iterative process was essential for identifying the core concept and ultimately formulating a theory. Fourth, the categories were presented in tables, with various comparisons illustrated through diagrams. During the selective coding stage, theoretical integration led to the identification of a crucial overarching factor. Finally, the researcher explained the process and flow of worldview transformation using a paradigm model to outline its factors and progression. Finally, a theory developed from these analytical processes was presented, synthesizing the findings into a coherent framework.

Analytical Process Leading to a Theory of Worldview Transformation

The core concept identified in this study is Experiencing God through the Word, which emerged as the key to the worldview transformation of North Korean defector Christians after their initial encounter with God at the stage of conversion. While the researcher initially expected a core concept similar to this finding, the participants' testimonies often deviated from these assumptions, leading the researcher to set aside prior expectations and remain fully open to the final results.

The following summarizes the process of analysis. First, the analysis revealed that participants suffered from trauma and crisis-induced challenges, including mental and emotional struggles stemming from the falsity, failure, and resulting hardships of the North Korean regime. It was observed that, to varying degrees, all participants shared worldview patterns common to North Koreans. While these difficulties ultimately contributed to their conversion, they also acted as obstacles to their continued worldview transformation in their walk with the LORD. Notably, 30 percent of the participants had already been exposed to Christian influences while still in North Korea, whether through gospel broadcasts, visits to China, Christian parental guidance, or God's supernatural intervention.

Second, all 20 participants reported having personal encounters with God at the time of their conversion. These experiences played a critical role in their worldview transformation, as they came to know and experience God's loving nature and presence, opened their hearts to be cleansed from sin, and received him as their Savior and LORD. Additionally, for those who struggled to find direction in life, the realization of God's will, calling, and guidance had a profound impact on their conversion. Furthermore, 80 percent of the participants indicated that their conversion was motivated by communal factors, as their felt needs were met through interactions with the Christian community. Moreover, not all participants experienced conversion as a shift from atheism or Kimilsungism to Christianity. For some, the transformation was more internal, as they already perceived God's presence in their worldview prior to conversion.

Conclusion

Third, the participants demonstrated significant changes in their understanding of God and their self-perception, often accompanied by new emotional experiences immediately following their conversion. As a result, their lifestyles and life goals shifted, becoming more God-centered and oriented toward the kingdom of God.

Fourth, although the participants' allegiance transitioned from the Kim family in North Korea to themselves and ultimately to Jesus Christ after conversion, the research revealed that 95 percent of them still had a limited understanding of God, self, and the kingdom. Consequently, their struggles in submitting to God's lordship over certain areas—such as a critical spirit, unforgiveness, and the idolization of missions in North Korea, and self—emerged as significant challenges. Additionally, 90 percent of participants continued to experience mental, emotional, and relational difficulties, with 60 percent reporting relational difficulties and 55 percent identifying anger, bitterness, fear, and unresolved pain as key issues. Beyond these personal struggles, 55 percent of participants also recognized remnants of North Korean ideological influences, such as self-reliance and humanism rooted in Juche, as obstacles to their worldview transformation.

Fifth, participants experienced God's intervention in their lives during times of personal devotion, particularly through reading Scripture and prayer. They also encountered the Holy Spirit's work in various ways, including hearing God's voice, receiving visions, and experiencing both physical and inner healing. Through these encounters, God imparted enlightenment and knowledge of himself and his will, often in the form of revelatory insights, corrections, and guidance. When he revealed himself as loving, forgiving, present with them, answering their prayers, and calling them to his kingdom, they responded with overwhelming gratitude. God also provided corrective guidance, convicting them of sin, while his Word shaped their perspectives, directed their daily lives, and deepened their relationship with him.

Sixth, in response to this divine revelation, some participants repented of sins such as misplaced priorities, lack of trust in God, self-righteousness, and immorality. Others experienced challenges or developed a longing for sanctification, a deeper relationship with God, and alignment with his kingdom. Although their responses varied, God's overarching purpose remained the same—to draw them closer to him until they became united in his Word. The research further revealed that Juche ideology, unresolved issues of lordship, and lingering struggles with criticism, anger, and hatred served as significant barriers to fully embracing God's Word. However, for those who remained open to deepening their relationship with God through Scripture and prayer, the experience of encountering him became profound. As they persevered in prayer, God continued to reveal more of himself, leading some participants to an ongoing process of internalization, in which his Word took root in their hearts, and his rule and reign became firmly established in their lives. This transformation was often evident to those around them.

Seventh, the contributing factors and process of worldview transformation, as previously explained, all point to a central theme: for God's Word to take root and his lordship to become manifest in the participants' lives, they needed to personally encounter him and allow him to enter deeper into their hearts. Thus, the core concept that emerged was *Experiencing God through the Word*. The theory constructed from this study's findings remains as previously described, emphasizing the participants' personal relationship with God as the driving force behind their transformation. This process involves internalizing the Word, persevering in prayer, and experiencing God in a profound way, leading to unity with his Word. As a result, the establishment of God's Word and his lordship in their lives becomes evident and often recognized by those around them.

Discussions on Previous Studies of North Korean Defectors

This section examines three recent studies on North Korean defectors that employed the Grounded Theory methodology: Seong Jong Joo's *A Grounded Theory on the Commitment of North Korean Defectors to Evangelical Christianity's Ministry*,[1] Jae Hwan Lim's "A Study on the Conversion Process Model of North Korean Defectors Based on Suffering-Overcoming: Application of Grounded Theory" (June 2021),[2] and Oh Sung Kwon's "A Case Study on the Conversion Process of North Korean Defectors Focusing on the Help and Realization of Transcendental Beings" (December 2021).[3]

Seong Jong Joo's *A Grounded Theory on the Commitment of North Korean Defectors to Evangelical Christianity's Ministry* was the first study to explore the commitment of North Korean defectors to Christian ministry using Grounded Theory methodology. Data was collected from 31 ministers

---

1. Jong Joo Seong, *A Research Methodology*.
2. Jae Hwan Lim, "Conversion Process Model."
3. Oh Sung Kwon, "Transcendental Beings."

Conclusion

and seminary students, and through detailed analysis, their commitment process was categorized into nine stages. The study identified *hardship* as the core concept, demonstrating that God, sovereign over all circumstances, powerfully intervened in the participants' lives through their hardships, refining and strengthening both their conversion and commitment. In this sense, their hard journey was understood as a gift from God. Additionally, the study highlighted the unique challenges faced by defectors in South Korea, where they encountered worldview and cultural conflicts. Based on these findings, Joo suggested that South Korean churches should seek to understand the biblical significance of the defectors' hardships and commitment, open doors for their ministry, and develop partnerships, all while approaching their experiences with humility.

In Joo's findings, the primary factors for the participants' conversion were identified as *God's Word* (48 percent) and *Spiritual Experiences* (23 percent). In the present study identifies *Experiencing God through the Word* as the central factor in worldview transformation. The core concept of hardship, identified in Joo's research, is also a significant conversion factor in this study. However, hardship is often assumed to be a common experience among all North Korean defectors, given the risks associated with their escape and their vulnerability to persecution and exploitation in transit countries. Yet, as illustrated by Participant NM's case, hardship is not necessarily defined by external dangers. While living in a transit nation, NM recalled this period as the happiest time of his life, as he experienced the love of a spiritual family, having previously been a *kotjebi* (a homeless child) with no family in North Korea. His greatest hardship was not physical danger but the mental and emotional burden of witnessing the deaths of numerous innocent children, including his own siblings, due to starvation and accidents.

Joo's research offers valuable insights into the challenges faced by defector ministers and the nature of their commitment. South Korean Christians and churches must attentively listen to the struggles defectors encounter in their commitment process to better understand how to support them.

Jae Hwan Lim's study, "A Study on the Conversion Process Model of North Korean Defectors Based on Suffering-Overcoming: Application of Grounded Theory," introduces a new model of conversion for North Korean defectors, building on Chang Sup Kang's analytical framework for the conversion of Chinese students in South Korea. Data was collected from

20 defectors who converted to Christianity in various contexts, including China, Southeast Asia, Russia, and South Korea. The analysis sought to identify the factors influencing their conversion process and categorize them using Paul Hiebert's three mental dimensions and Eiko Takamizawa's three analytic dimensions. The findings indicate that the primary factor in the participants' conversion was *Encounter with God*—an experiential dimension through which they came to faith.

By integrating these findings, Lim developed the *Hardship-Overcoming* model to describe the conversion process of North Korean defectors. His study explains that defectors fled North Korea in search of a better life but continued to experience hardship in transit nations. Even after arriving in South Korea, many still faced significant mental and emotional struggles despite no longer experiencing material deprivation. However, through *encountering God*, they were able to overcome these hardships, experience transformation, and even commit their lives to the LORD. Based on this study, Lim emphasizes the need for South Korean churches to provide continuous presence, support, and healing programs tailored to defectors' unique hardships. He also suggests the development of a new model of gospel presentation based on the Hardship-Overcoming framework, arguing that traditional conversion models such as those of Lewis Rambo and Edwin Starbuck, while useful, may not fully explain the conversion experiences of defectors, who have endured prolonged and extreme suffering.

This study identifies *Encounter with God* as the primary factor in participants' conversion, based on an analysis of Lim's findings. This encounter occurred in various ways, such as through experiencing Christ's love in the Christian community, receiving answered prayers, finding comfort and empowerment in reading the Bible, understanding God's will, and experiencing the Holy Spirit's saving intervention during times of distress. Lim's findings regarding transformation after conversion—particularly in terms of lifestyle changes, new life goals, and shifts in attitude toward others—align closely with the themes identified in this study. His Hardship-Overcoming model provides valuable insights into the conversion process of North Korean defectors, offering a nuanced perspective on their journey to faith.

Kwon's study, "A Case Study on the Conversion Process of North Korean Defectors Focusing on the Help and Realization of Transcendental Beings" (December 2021), differs in methodology but is notable for its emphasis on the role of a transcendental being in the conversion process of North Korean defectors. His research identifies five key themes: defectors' initial departure from North Korea in search of a better life, their struggles with economic hardship, their exposure to new cultures and encounters with missionaries and pastors in transit nations, their experience of divine help, and their eventual understanding of the transcendental being through the Bible, as explained by Christian mentors.

A crucial insight from Kwon's study is that defectors could have remained within the North Korean system without ever becoming aware of the transcendental being. However, it was through their experiences of divine help during their escape and extreme hardships in transit nations that they became aware of God's presence. Their encounters with Christian communities further reinforced this awareness, as they witnessed tangible expressions of love and care. These themes align with this study's findings, particularly regarding hardship as a factor in disillusionment with previously trusted ideologies, the vulnerability of defectors due to lack of safety and provision, and the role of God's common grace in leading them toward faith. Most significantly, the theme of encountering a transcendent being is central to both studies.

In summary, while each of these studies focuses on different aspects of North Korean defectors' conversion and commitment—drawing from distinct participant groups and research approaches—their core themes are interconnected. The insights gained from these studies contribute to a deeper understanding of the conversion process, the challenges faced by defectors, and God's active involvement in their transformation. This research on worldview transformation greatly benefits from the contributions of these previous studies and appreciates the valuable perspectives they offer.

Missiological Implications

North Korean defectors were bound by Juche for their lifetime in North Korea. However, going through the Arduous March, many were disillusioned by the regime and opened their hearts to receive the gospel that was shared by Christians, whether inside North Korea or in transit nations. Encountering God and experiencing conversion was a profound and transformative experience. However, becoming a genuine Christian entails a separate journey and set of challenges. It is worth noting that while many defectors may have had a conversion experience, a significant number have discontinued their involvement with the church after arriving in South Korea for various reasons. This highlights the complexity and unique circumstances faced by North Korean defectors as they navigate their faith journey in a new environment.

This research initially aimed to explore the factors influencing the worldview transformation of defector Christians, especially those who have undergone significant changes, such as ministers. The goal was to help nominal or spiritually weak defector Christians grow based on the research findings. However, in the long run, participants are more likely to interact with fellow Christians than with ministers. In their interactions, a lack of genuine transformation could lead to more believers without true change. Thomas A. Tarrants pointed out that Jesus did not call us to "make converts" but to "make disciples," meaning the goal is not just conversion but transformation through discipleship.[4] Discipleship involves guiding others to develop a personal relationship with God, leading to real character and behavioral change—something crucial for both defector and South Korean Christians.

That being said, for many defectors, once their basic needs are met and they find stability in their new environment, they may no longer feel the urgency for continued spiritual growth, resulting in limited transformation. This phenomenon is reflected in Eui-Hyuck Kim's article, "Christian Missions for North Korean Migrants in the COVID-19 Era." He identified three key stages in defectors' departure from Christianity: transitioning to regional residency after leaving Hanawon, settling in the South and attending church for 3 to 4 years, and finally adjusting to South Korean society. This data indicates that even though some individuals claim to believe in God, they may still maintain control as the masters of their own lives. Once their desires are fulfilled, their lives may revert to a state similar to before, lacking true transformation or genuine surrender to God's authority. This limitation in spiritual growth is further evidenced by the persistence of ideological elements from their past. Even after leaving North Korea for China, Kimilsungism may fade, but elements of Juche ideology and communism often persist. Additionally, exposure to capitalism and freedom outside of North Korea can lead defectors to adopt humanism and concepts like original sin in the South.

We recognize that both South Korean Christians and defector Christians alike require a deepened and broadened understanding of God and his lordship. Especially, as Participant KF confessed about the purpose and

---

4. Tarrants, "Go, Make Disciples."

Conclusion

calling of defectors, they are not only recipients of God's grace but also bear a prophetic calling for the South Korean church, and by extension, the global church. To be such a tool for the kingdom, their worldview and the lordship of Jesus Christ need to be expanded, and they need to be able to think beyond the necessities of life. Otherwise, they are likely to limit the scope of their calling. It is not necessarily their misconception about Christ or Christianity but their lack of knowledge of God, the self, and the kingdom, which needs growth and expansion.

A key dynamic in the relationship between defectors and the church is their disappointment with the church's inability to present a vision of faith that offers a meaningful and transformative alternative to the prevailing values of South Korean society. The South Korean church must reflect on its practices to cultivate a faith that stands apart from societal norms. The church must not only provide comprehensive support to defectors by addressing their immediate practical needs but also embark on a deeper exploration of the essence of Christian faith and its transformative meaning. This endeavor requires a collaborative effort, drawing from both historical and theoretical perspectives, to ensure that the faith imparted is not merely superficial but deeply rooted in theological understanding, ultimately fostering lasting spiritual growth and integration within the broader ecclesial context.

In summary, recent global challenges, such as the lasting impacts of the COVID-19 pandemic, have profoundly transformed our lives challenging our worldviews and pushing us to confront a new reality. These disruptions have provided a unique opportunity for introspection and a reevaluation of the core aspects of our Christian faith. We are prompted to ask critical questions about who God truly is, our identity in him, and the depth of his lordship in our lives. Moreover, we are called to reflect on how we can actively manifest God's kingdom in this new season.

For both defectors and South Korean Christians, as one body in Christ Jesus, looking to the life of Jesus Christ provides a powerful and transformative model for our own lives as believers. Additionally, every member of the body of Christ, along with the fivefold ministry—apostles, prophets, evangelists, pastors, and teachers—should strive to be equipped "for works of service to build up his body on the earth" (Eph 4:12). We strive for maturity, "speaking the truth in love and attaining unity in the faith and the knowledge of the Son of God" (Eph 4:13). As each part fulfills its role, the whole body grows from God and "builds itself up in love" (Eph 4:16).

Suggestions for Further Studies

One of the suggestions for further studies is to examine the worldview of defector Christians, focusing on their cognitive, affective, and evaluative assumptions to assess whether these align with the gospel of Jesus Christ. If discrepancies are found, further research could explore the values and systems shaping their worldview, aiming to identify areas where these influences can be replaced with the truth of the gospel. Understanding these underlying assumptions would provide deeper insight into the spiritual formation of defectors and the factors that either hinder or facilitate their transformation.

Second, it is essential to explore effective ways to engage defectors with a genuine, balanced, and congruent biblical worldview, whether through online or offline means. A worldview is continuously shaped and transformed through coherent and explicit life narratives, influencing both individuals and society. Similarly, the worldview transformation of North Korean defectors, who are already present among us, can be facilitated through narratives that articulate the essence of life and the biblical worldview more clearly. This transformation, however, cannot be achieved merely through intellectual discourse or doctrinal instruction. It must be accompanied by the demonstration of a genuine Christian life, as exemplified in the life of Jesus Christ. By living out the gospel in a way that is both authentic and relational, believers can create an environment where defectors not only hear biblical truth but also witness its transformative power firsthand.

Appendix A
Consent Form

Title of Research: Study on the Worldview Transformation of North Korean Defector Christians in South Korea

1. I have read the instructions and the informed consent form related to the study conducted by the researcher.
2. I have been informed of the benefits and risks, and I am satisfied with the answers provided to my questions.
3. I voluntarily agree to participate in this research.
4. I agree that the research will collect data in accordance with the regulations of the Institutional Review Board (IRB).
5. I agree that the person designated by the researcher will conduct the study and maintain the results, and that the IRB, the school, and any institution commissioned by the Department of Health and Welfare may review the study, including any data related to me.
6. I understand that I may withdraw from the research at any time without any harm or penalty.
7. My signature confirms that I have received the consent form and will keep it until the completion of the study.

Participant Name:
Signature:
Date:

Appendix B
Demographic Questionnaire

Name:

1. How long have you been in Korea?
2. How long did you stay in the transit nation(s) before arriving in Korea?
3. When did you become a Christian?
4. When were you baptized?
5. Which church or Christian organization are you currently part of?
6. Have you received any training from a church or Christian organization that has helped shape your Biblical worldview?

Bibliography

Adams, Nicholas. Review of Robert R. Williams, *Hegel on the Proofs and the Personhood of God: Studies in Hegel's Logic and Studies and Philosophy of Religion*. Notre Dame Philosophical Reviews. https://ndpr.nd.edu/reviews/hegel-on-the-proofs-and-the-personhood-of-god-studies-in-hegels-logic-and-philosophy-of-religion/. Accessed March 9, 2023.
Adventist News. "Status of North Korean Religion and Settlement of North Korean Refugees." March 16, 2022. http://www.sdanews.org/news/articleView.html?idxno=13968. Accessed January 21, 2023.
Ahn, Heui Yeol. "A Study of the Cross-Cultural Missionary Movement of the Baptist Church in Korea." ThM thesis, Southwestern Baptist Theological Seminary, 1995.
Ahn, Jum Shik. *Worldview, Religion, Culture*. Seoul: Joy, 2008.
Ahn, Ran Hee. "Christian Life and Ministry of North Korean Refugees: Focused on 1992–2014." MDiv thesis, Seoul Theological University, 2015.
Anderson, Tawa J., W. Michael Clark, and David K. Naugle. *An Introduction to Christian Worldview: Pursuing God's Perspective in a Pluralistic World*. London: Inter-Varsity, 2017.
Armstrong, Charles K. *The North Korean Revolution, 1945–1950*. Ithaca, NY: Cornell University Press, 2003.
Balas, Baran. "What Do Marx and Hegel in Common." *The Collector*, Dec. 15, 2022. https://www.thecollector.com/what-do-hegel-and-marx-have-in-common/. Accessed May 4, 2023.
Behnke, Alison. *Kim Jong Il's North Korea*. Minneapolis: Lerner, 2008.
Burke, Trevor J., and Andrew E. Hill, eds. *New Dictionary of Biblical Theology*. Downers Grove, IL: InterVarsity, 2000. s.v. "Creation."
Bloesch, Donald G. "The Meaning of Conversion." *Christianity Today*, May 24, 1968. https://www.christianitytoday.com/ct/1968/may-24/meaning-of-conversion.html. Accessed January 16, 2023.
Bosch, David. *Transforming Mission: Paradigm Shifts in Theology of Mission*. American Society of Missiology Series 16. Maryknoll, NY: Orbis, 2010.

Bibliography

Carswell, J. Jamieson. "materialism." *Encyclopedia Britannica*. Apr. 20, 2023. https://www.britannica.com/topic/materialism-philosophy.

Charmaz, Kathy. *Constructing Grounded Theory: A Practical Guide Through Qualitative Analysis*. London: Sage, 2006.

Christianity Daily. "99.6 % of Defectors Couldn't Do Religious Activities Freely in North Korea." Oct. 24, 2019. https://kr.christianitydaily.com/articles. Accessed August 26, 2024.

Chung, Hyung Shin. "North Korean Mission and Unification with Focus on North Korean Defector Church." *Christiantoday*, June 14, 2022. http://www.christiantoday.co.kr/news/348191, Accessed January 21, 2023.

Chung, Woo Gon. "National Development Strategy Under the Kim Jong Il Regime: Building a Kangsong Taeguk (Strong and Prosperous Nation)." *Korea and International Politics* 20, no. 4 (2004) 35–66. https://www.kci.go.kr/kciportal/ci/sereArticleSearch/ciSereArtiView.kci?sereArticleSearchBean.artiId=ART001107228. Accessed Mar. 10, 2023.

"Conversion." In *Dictionary of Methodism in Britain and Ireland*. Accessed July 23, 2023. https://www.dmbi.online/index.php?do=app.entry&id=690.

Corbin, Juliet, and Anselm Strauss. *Basics of Qualitative Research* 3e. Thousand Oaks, CA: Sage, 2008.

Cresswell, John W. *Qualitative Inquiry & Research Design: Choosing Among Five Approaches*. London: Sage, 2007.

Creswell, John W., and Cheryl N. Poth. *Qualitative Inquiry & Research Design: Choosing Among Five Approaches*. 4th ed. Thousand Oaks, CA: Sage, 2018.

English, John. *Spiritual Intimacy and Community: An Ignatian View of the Small Faith Community*. Mahwah, NJ: Paulist, 1992.

Erickson, Milliard J. *Christian Theology*. Grand Rapids: Baker Academic, 1983.

Fee, Gordon D. *Paul, the Spirit and the People of God*. Peabody, MA: Hendrickson, 1996.

Fesko, J. V. *The Fruit of the Spirit Is . . .* Grange Close, UK: Evangelical Press, 2011. Internet Archive. https://archive.org/details/fruitofspiritisoooofesk/mode/2up?view=theater. Accessed February 27, 2023.

Goheen, Michael W., and Craig G. Bartholomew. *Living at the Crossroads: An Introduction to Christian Worldview*. Grand Rapids: Baker Academic, 2008.

Golafshani, Nahid "Understanding Reliability and Validity in Qualitative Research." *The Qualitative Report* 8.4 (2003). 597–607. https://www.researchgate.net/publication/313551785_Understanding_reliability_and_validity_in_qualitative_research. Accessed July 6, 2023.

Gyeongnam University Research Institution for Far Eastern Affairs. "National Development Strategy Under the Kim Jong Il Regime: Building a Kangsong Taeguk (Strong and Prosperous Nation)." *Korea and International Politics* 20.4 (2004) 35–66.

Harper, Colin M. "Discovering the Truth within Falsehood: Colin M. Harper on the Non-reductive Atheism of Ludwig Feuerbach." *Philosophy Now* 7 (Fall 1993). https://philosophynow.org/issues/17/Discovering_the_Truth_within_falsehood, Accessed March 9, 2023.

Hiebert, Paul G. *Transforming Worldviews: An Anthropological Understanding of How People Change*. Grand Rapids: Baker Academic, 2008.

Hoare, James E. "Juche." In *Historical Dictionary of the Democratic People's Republic of Korea*. Lanham, MD: Scarecrow, 2012.

Bibliography

"Hwang Jang-yop." *Wikipedia: The Free Encyclopedia.* Last modified June 14, 2024. https://en.wikipedia.org/wiki/Hwang_Jang-yop. Accessed August 2, 2023.

Institute for Unification Education. *Understanding North Korea 2007.* Seoul: Ministry of Unification, 2007. 30. https://www.unikorea.go.kr/books/understand/understand/ebook/under_NK_2007/assets/contents/download.pdf. Accessed January 27, 2023.

Jeon, Woo Taek, Shi Eun Yu, and Yun Woo Lee. "The Patterns and Formation of National Identity among North Korean Refugees in South Korea: A Grounded Theory Study." *International Journal of Korean Unification Studies* 20.2 (2011) 1–35.

Jo, Yong Kwan, and Byung Ro Kim. *One Step Toward North Korea.* Kyunggi-do: YWAM, 2006.

Joo, Seong Jong. *A Research Methodology of Mission for North Korea: A Ground Theory on the Commitment of North Korean Defectors to Evangelical Christianity's Ministry.* Seoul: CLC, 2022.

Jun, Myung-Hee, Sook Hee Jung, et al. "A Qualitative Study Toward Understanding the Process of Religious Experiences of Christian North Korean Defectors: Through the Grounded Theory Approach." *Korean Journal of Christian Counseling* 30, no. 4 (2016) 173–207.

Jun, Myung-Hee, Jung A Park, and Seong Hwi Cho. "A Phenomenological Study Toward Understanding the Process of Religious Conversion of Christian Young Adults from North Korea: Through the Phenomenological Approach." *Korean Journal of Christian Counseling & Psychology* 29 no. 3 (2018) 219–250.

Kang, Chang Seop. "Conversion of Chinese Student in Korea to Evangelical Christianity: Factors, Process, and Types." PhD diss., Torch Trinity Graduate University, 2016.

———. *Transforming Research Methodology for Missiology: Practical Guide Through Grounded Theory.* Seoul: CLC, 2018.

Kang, Kyung Mi. "North Korean Defectors' Mal-Adjustment to South Korean Churches: Why?" *Church Planting* 49 (Summer 2018) 197–216.

———. "Worldview of North Korea and Gospel's Spiritual World." *North Korean Church* 5, no. 4 (Winter 2007) 72–85.

Kavanaugh, John Francis. *Following Christ in a Consumer Society: The Spirituality of Cultural Resistance.* Maryknoll, NY: Orbis, 1981. Internet Archive. https://archive.org/details/followingchristi00john/mode/2up?view=theater. Accessed March 27, 2023.

KBS World. "N. Korean Leader Mentions 'Arduous Journey.'" Apr. 22, 2021, http://world.kbs.co.kr/service/contents_view.htm?lang=e&board_seq=402037. Accessed June 30, 2023.

KBS World Radio. "North Korean Leader: Juche (Self-Reliance) Ideology." https://world.kbs.co.kr/special/northkorea/contents/archives/supreme_leader/ideology.htm?lang=e. Accessed May 4, 2023.

Kearney, Michael. *World View.* Chandler & Sharp Publications in Anthropology and Related Fields. Novato, CA: Chandler & Sharp, 2001.

Kenny, Méabh, and Robert Fourie. "Contrasting Classic, Straussian, and Constructivist Grounded Theory: Methodological and Philosophical Conflicts." https://nsuworks.nova.edu/cgi/viewcontent.cgi?article=2251&context=tqr. Accessed July 22, 2023.

Kent State University. "Statistics & Qualitative Data Analysis Software: About NVIVO." https://libguides.library.kent.edu/statconsulting/NVivo

Kim, Byung Ro. "Religiosity of North Korean Society: Comparison of religious forms between Juche Ideology and Christianity." *Unification Research Center Studies Edition* 00–04 (February 2000) 1.

BIBLIOGRAPHY

———. *The Study on the Internalization of Juche Ideology*. Seoul: Korean Unification Study Institution, 1994. https://lib.uniedu.go.kr/libeka/elec/0000595482.pdf.

Kim, Eui-Hyuck. "Christian Missions for North Korean Migrants in the COVID-19 Era." *Theology of Mission* 60 (2020) 84–112.

———. "Crossing the Divide and Crossing the Boundary: Who Are North Korean Refugees?" *The Christian Literature Society of Korea* 755 (November 2021): 177. https://www.dbpia.co.kr/journal/articleDetail?nodeId=NODE10620654. Accessed May 4, 2023.

———. "North Korean Migrants' Church Experiences in South Korea: New Place, Old Issues." PhD diss., Fuller Theological Seminary, 2019.

———. "Understanding North Korean Defectors and Korean Church 03: Settlement Story in the Lower Part of the Unfamiliar and Rough Neighborhood." *Christian Thought* 753 (2021) 168–80. https://www.dbpia.co.kr/journal/articleDetail?nodeId=NODE10599344%20175. Accessed May 4, 2023.

Kim, Gwang Myung. "Research on the Mission Strategies for the 'Juche Ideolized' North Korean Defectors." MA diss., Soongsil University Graduate School of Industry, 2000.

Kim, Hak-Kyu. *The Unification Strategy of the North Korean Regime: National Development Strategy Under Kim Jong Il's Reign*. Seoul: Na-Nam, 2006.

Kim, Il Sung. *Answers to the Foreign Reporters*. Vol. 3 (1976–1982). Pyongyang: Rodongdang, 1983. https://lib.uniedu.go.kr/library/original/view?mGubun=1&dataTypes=&format=list&pageSize=30&method=KEYWORD&fields=ALL&keywords=%EC%99%B8%EA%B5%AD%EA%B8%B0%EC%9E%90%EB%93%A4%EC%9D%B4&x=22&y=4&uid=CAT-20170600000000322.

Kim, Jeong Gwon, and James B. Torrance. "An Anthropological Understanding of Juche Ideology and Its Background." *Journal of Christian Philosophy* 15.1 (2012) 11–45.

Kim, Jin-Man. "The Analysis on Internalization-mechanism in the Epistemology of Juche ideology." *Journal of Ethics* 1.62 (2006) 352–353.

Kim, Jong Il. "On Some Questions in Understanding Juche Philosophy." *Marxists Internet Archive* (1974) 1–8. https://www.marxists.org/archive/kim-jong-il/works/On-Some-Questions-In-Understanding-The-Juche-Philosophy.pdf, Accessed March 7, 2023.

Kim, Jung Ho. ed. *The Issues of the Organizations in Relation to North Korean Defectors and Seeking for Desirable Roles*. Seoul: Jayukiupwon, 2011.

Kim, Jung Il. *On the Juche Philosophy*. Pyongyang: Rodongdang, 1982.

Kim, Seung Kook. "Religious Worldview and Experience in North Korea: Focused on the Experiences of North Korean Christians." PhD diss., Hanil University & Presbyterian Theological Seminary, 2021.

Kim, Sung Kook. "A Missiological Study on the Conversion of North Korean Defectors to Christianity." PhD diss., Asian Center for Theological Studies and Mission, 2005.

Kim, Yong Seok. "A Study on the Church Planting Strategy for North Korean Refugees: Missiological Analysis of Adaptation and Ministry of North Korean Refugees." PhD diss., International Theological Seminary, 2009.

King, Robert. "Number of North Korean Defectors Declines." *The Peninsula*, posted Feb. 19, 2020. https://keia.org/the-peninsula/number-of-north-korean-defectors-declines/. Accessed May 4, 2023.

Korea Christian Research Institution. "The Present Status of Religious of North Korean Refugees: 20 years Statistics of North Korean Refugees." Dec. 31, 2014. http://www.kpastors.org/pds/bbs/board.php?bo_table=sub01_01&wr_id=151. Accessed November 27, 2023.

Bibliography

Korea Institute for National Unification. *White Paper on Human Rights in North Korea 2020*. Seoul: Korea Institute for National Unification, 2020.

Korea JoongAng Daily. "U.S. Takes North Refugee as South's Safe-Haven Status Questioned." Nov. 1, 2022. https://koreajoongangdaily.joins.com/2022/11/01/national/northKorea/Korea-North-Korea-North-Korean-Human-Rights-Act/20221101184912547.html. Accessed July 14, 2023.

Korea Social Science Institute. "North Korean Defectors Survey 2011." *North Korean Defectors Survey*. Seoul: Korea Social Science Institute, 2011.

Korea Worldview Education Center. *A Bible Study in the Book of Philippians*. Seoul: Korea Worldview Education Center, 2023.

Kraft, Charles H. *Anthropology for Christian Witness*. Maryknoll, NY: Orbis, 1997.

———. *Christianity in Culture: A Study in Dynamic Biblical Theologizing in Cross-Cultural Perspective*. Maryknoll, NY: Orbis, 2005.

Kraft, Charles H., Christie Varney, and Ellen Kearney. *Christianity with Power: Your Worldview and Your Experience of the Supernatural*. Ann Arbor, MI: Servant Publications, 1989.

Kretzschmar, Louise. "Spirituality and Transformation in Africa." *Mission Studies* 28.2 (2011) 153–78.

Kwon, Hee Jung. "North Korean Mission and Defector Refugees." *Theology Study* 7.2 (2018) 29.

———. "The Formation and Process of Internalizing Worldview in North Korea." PhD diss., Yonsei University, 2015.

Kwon, Oh Sung. "A Case Study on the Conversion Process of North Korean Defectors Focusing on the Help and Realization of Transcendental Beings." PhD diss., Soongshil University, 2021.

Lankov, Andrei. "A Time When North Korean Defectors Disappeared." *Radio Free Asia*, Sept. 8, 2022. https://www.rfa.org/korean/commentary/lankov/alcu-09082022111129.html. Accessed November 19, 2022.

Lee, Jong Hun. "A Study on the Christianity of North Korean Defectors: Focused on House Church Leaders." MDiv thesis, Baekseok University, 2009.

Lee, Sang Jin. "Churches' Tasks on North Korea Mission." *Korean Christian World*, June 26, 2018.

Leung, Lawrence. "Validity, Reliability, and Generalizability in Qualitative Research." https://www.ncbi.nlm.nih.gov/pmc/articles/PMC4535087/. Accessed July 6, 2023.

Lim, Jae Wan. "A Study on the Conversion Process Model of North Korean Defectors Based on the Suffering-Overcoming: Application of Grounded Theory." PhD diss., Soongshil University, 2021.

Liulevicius, Vejas. "Marx, Engels, the Rise of Communism." *Wondrium Daily*, June 16, 2020. https://www.wondriumdaily.com/marx-engels-and-the-rise-of-communism/. Accessed March 9, 2023. (Note: URL no longer active)

"Materialistic." In *American Heritage Dictionary of the English Language*. 5th ed., s.v. "materialistic." https://www.thefreedictionary.com/materialistic. Accessed March 5, 2023.

"Materialistic." In *The American Heritage Roget's Thesaurus*. from https://www.thefreedictionary.com/materialistic. Accessed March 5, 2023.

"Migrant." In *Cambridge Dictionary*. https://dictionary.cambridge.org/ko/%EC%82%AC%EC%A0%84/%EC%98%81%EC%96%B4/migrant. Accessed November 25, 2022.

Bibliography

Ministry of National Unification and Education. *Understanding North Korea 2013*. Seoul: Education Development Division, 2013.

Ministry of Unification. "Life Review Session." https://nkinfo.unikorea.go.kr/nkp/knwldg/view/knwldg.do;jsessionid=FAlWqdAdxF67_phsAoW3lCQfKoGR9B2LMjwqXe6B.ins22?menuId=NK_KNWLDG_DICARY&knwldgNo=256. Accessed September 1, 2023.

———. "Recent Status." https://www.unikorea.go.kr/unikorea/business/NKDefectorsPolicy/status/lately/. Accessed May 4, 2023.

———. "South Korean Government's Settlement Support for NK Defectors." http://www.unikorea.go.kr/unikorea/business/NKDefectorsPolicy/settlement/System/. Accessed May 4, 2023.

———. "Ten Principles for the Establishment of the One-Ideology System." https://nkinfo.unikorea.go.kr/nkp/term/viewNkKnwldgDicary.do?pageIndex=1&dicaryId=144. Accessed May 4, 2023.

The Mission. "Disillusioned with the Church, Which Is Expected to Be the Messenger of the Gospel but Instead Attempts to Bind Them Through Financial Means." Mar 29, 2023. https://www.themission.co.kr/news/articleView.html?idxno=62092. Accessed Jul. 14, 2023.

Mitias, Michael H. "Marx and the Human Individual." *Studies in Soviet Thought* 12.3 (1972) 245–54. https://www.jstor.org/stable/20098506. Accessed May 4, 2023.

Moon, Kwang Cheol. "A Strategy for Mission to North Korean Defectors." MDiv thesis, Asia United Theological University, 2005.

Nam, In Soo. "South Korean Government's Settlement Policy for North Korean Defectors and Their Adjustment Problems." *Law Research* 44.2 (2014) 371.

Oh, Woon Hak. "Study of Changes in the Worldviews of North Korean Defectors." MA thesis, Chong Shin University, Seoul, 1999.

Oliver, Alvyn P. "The Meaning of Conversion." *Evangelical Quarterly* 15 (1943) 26–34.

"On the Juche Idea." *Wikipedia: The Free Encyclopedia*. Last modified March 9, 2024. https://en.wikipedia.org/wiki/On_the_Juche_Idea. Accessed August 30, 2024

Packer, J. I. *Knowing God*. Downers Grove, IL: Intervarsity,1973.

———. *Rediscovering Holiness*. Ann Arbor, MI: Servant Publications, 1992. Internet Archive. https://archive.org/details/rediscoveringholoooopack/page/n5/mode/2up?view=theater. Accessed April 21, 2023.

Park, Eun Hye. "Identity Change Process of North Korean Defectors: Mission of Church." MDiv thesis, Westminster Graduate School of Theology, 2016.

Park, Myung Kyu, Byung Ro Kim, et al. *North Korean Diaspora: Migration to Overseas and the Settlement Situation of North Korean People*. Seoul: Seoul National University Research Institute for Peaceful Unification, 2011.

Park, Ye Young. (Oh, Teresa.) "A Study on the Conversion Experience of the North Korean Christian Refugees." In *People Who Stand Together on the Way to Unification 5-'Reconciliation and Embracing,'* edited by Kee Woo Lee. Seoul: Good Tidings, 2016. 94–110.

Park, Young-Hwan, "The Actual Conditions of Faith of North Korean Defectors in South Korea and Its Influence." *Korean Christian Social Welfare Research* 20.2 (2017) 27–49.

Park, Young-Tae. "The Phenomenological Study on the Conversion Experience of North Korean Defectors." PhD diss., Baekseok University, 2008.

Peter, J. Williams. *Can We Trust the Gospels?* Wheaton, IL: Crossway, 2018.

Bibliography

Pickett, Fuchsia. *Cultivating the Gifts & Fruit of the Holy Spirit.* Lake Mary, FL: Charisma House, 2004. Internet Archive.

Plantinga Jr., Cornelius. *Not the Way It's Supposed to Be: A Breviary of Sin.* Grand Rapids: Eerdmans, 1995. Internet Archive. https://archive.org/details/notwayitssupposeooplan/mode/2up?view=theater. Accessed March 27, 2023.

Pyong, Sam Yong. "Worldview of North Korean Christians and Its Comparison with the Worldview of South Korean Christians." PhD diss., Yonsei University, 2022.

Radmacher, Earl D., ed. *Nelson's New Illustrated Bible Commentary: Spreading the Light of God's Word into Your Life.* Nashville: Nelson, 1999.

Rambo, Lewis R. "Psychology of Conversion." In *Handbook of Religious Conversion*, edited by H. Newton Malony, and Samuel Southard. Birmingham, AL: Religious Education, 1992. Internet Archive. https://archive.org/details/handbookofreligiooounse_h3h3/page/n7/mode/2up. Accessed March 12, 2023.

———. *Understanding Religious Conversion.* New Heaven: Yale University Press, 1993.

Rambo, Lewis R., and Charles E. Farhadian. "Converting: Stages of Religious Change." In *Religious Conversion: Contemporary Practices and Controversies,* edited by Christopher Lamb, and M. Darrol Bryant. 23–34. London: Cassell, 1999. Internet Archive. https://archive.org/details/religiousconversooounse_n4i7/page/n7/mode/2up. Accessed March 12, 2023.

Resis, Albert. "Vladimir Lenin." In *Encyclopedia Britannica.* Apr. 18, 2023. https://www.britannica.com/biography/Vladimir-Lenin. Accessed March 9, 2023.

Right to Remain News. "North Korea Refugees in the UK." Jun. 29, 2015. https://righttoremain.org.uk/north-korean-refugees-in-the-uk/. Accessed July 14, 2023.

Ryken, Philip Graham. *Christian Worldview: A Student's Guide,* edited by David S. Dockery. Wheaton, IL: Crossway, 2013.

Seo, Jae Jin. *Comparison Study between North Korean Marx-Leninism and Juche Ideology.* Seoul: Korean Unification Research Center, 2002. https://repo.kinu.or.kr/bitstream/2015.oak/666/1/0000597245.pdf. Accessed March 10, 2023.

Silverman, David. "Validity, Reliability, and Generalizability in Qualitative Research." *PubMed Central.* https://pmc.ncbi.nlm.nih.gov/articles/PMC4535087/?utm_source=chatgpt.com. Accessed January 29, 2025.

Sire, James W. *The Universe Next Door: A Basic Worldview Catalog.* 5th ed. Downers Grove, IL: IVP Academic, 2009.

Song, Young Sup. "Socio-cultural Factors Influencing the Conversion to Christianity among North Korean Refugees in South Korea." PhD diss., Trinity Evangelical Divinity School, 2011.

———. "Understanding North Korean Defectors in the View of Diaspora and Missional Meaning." *Korea Reformed Journal* 37 (2016) 131–158.

SPN Seoul Pyongyang News. "NKDB 'Summary of 2020 White Paper on North Korean Human Rights.'" Nov. 2, 2020. https://www.spnews.co.kr/news/articleView.html?idxno=33980, Accessed January 11, 2023.

Strauss, Anselm, and Juliet Corbin. *Basics of Qualitative Research: Grounded Theory Procedures and Techniques.* Newbury Park, CA: Sage, 1990.

———. *Basics of Qualitative Research: Techniques and Procedures for Development Grounded Theory.* Thousand Oaks, CA: Sage, 1998.

———. "Grounded Theory Methodology: An Overview." In *Strategies of Qualitative Inquiry,* edited by Norman K. Denzin and Yvonna S. Lincoln, 273–85. Thousand Oaks, CA: Sage, 1998.

Bibliography

Tarrants, Thomas A. "Go, Make Disciples of All Nations." Dec, 4, 2017. *C. S. Lewis Institute.* https://www.cslewisinstitute.org/resources/go-make-disciples-of-all-nations/.

"Ten Principles for the Establishment of a Monolithic Ideological System." *Wikipedia: The Free Encyclopedia.* https://en.wikiedia.org/wiki/Ten_Principles_for_the_Establishment_of_a_Monolithic_Ideological_System. Accessed August 30, 2024.

Thomas, Murray R. "The Democratic People's Republic of Korea (North Korea)." In *Schooling in East Asia: Forces of Change,* edited by Murray R. Thomas and Neville Postlethwaite, 133–51. London: Pergamon, 1983.

Torrey, Ben. "North Korean Migrants in South Korea: How Can the Korean Church Best Serve Them?" In *People Disrupted: Doing Mission Responsibly among Refugees and Migrants,* edited by Jinbong Kim, Dwight P. Baker, Jonathan J. Bonk, J. Nelson Jennings, and Jae Hoon Lee, 137–50. Pasadena, CA: Willian Carey Library, 2018.

UN Migration. "IOM Definition of 'Migrant.'" https://www.iom.int/about-migration.

The UN Refugee Agency. "'Refugees' and 'Migrants' Frequently Asked Questions (FAQs)." https://www.unhcr.or.kr/unhcr/program/board/detail.jsp?boardTypeID=8&searchSelect=&keyWord=&currentPage=1&menuID=&finishIsYN=&boardID=7687&boardCategory=%EA%B3%B5%EC%A7%80&mode=detail. Accessed November 25, 2022.

———. "What Is a Refugee?" https://www.unhcr.org/what-is-a-refugee.html. Accessed November 25, 2022.

Walsh, Brian J., and J. Richard Middleton. *The Transforming Vision.* Downers Grove, IL: InterVarsity, 1984.

Whitmarsh, Tim. "5–Ancient Greece: Atheism in History." In *Cambridge History of Atheism,* edited by Stephen Bullivant and Michael Ruse, 84–99. 2 vols. Cambridge: Cambridge University Press, 2021. https://www.cambridge.org/core/books/abs/cambridge-history-of-atheism/ancient-greece/E00F297306CF70DD76D6C4564326D684. Accessed March 5, 2023

Wright, John G. "Feuerbach: Philosopher of Materialism (Fall 1956)." *International Socialist Review* 17.4 (1956). https://www.marxists.org/history/etol/writers/wright/1956/xx/feuerbach.htm. Accessed May 4, 2023.

Yoo, Duk Ho. "A Study on the Evangelization Process of North Korean Defectors: Through Their Faith Experience." MDiv thesis, Yonsei University, 2022.

You, Jai Ryung. "A Study on Identity Reconstruction of North Korean Defectors through Faith: Focused on Korean Christian Church Ministry." PhD diss., Korea Baptist Theological University, 2023.

Young, Benjamin. "Understanding North Korea's 'Final Victory' and Why It Matters." *NK News,* Sept. 6, 2021. https://www.nknews.org/2021/09/understanding-north-koreas-final-victory-and-why-it-matters/. Accessed March 10, 2023.

Yu, Shi-Eun, Kyung-Ja Oh, et al. "A Qualitative Study of North Korean Refugees' Attitude Shifts: Focusing on Those in South Korea for Three Years." *Unification Research* 16.2 (2012) 67–120.

Yun, Il Hyuk. *The Reconstruction of Christian Worldview.* Seoul: Christian Literature Crusade, 2008.

Yung, Hwa Ryong. "North Korean Refugee Crisis: A Missional Analysis." *Missiology: An International Revi*ew 41.4 (2013) 42–58.

www.ingramcontent.com/pod-product-compliance
Lightning Source LLC
Chambersburg PA
CBHW051739230426
43670CB00012B/2084